AMS PRESS
NEW YORK

Reprinted from the edition of 1910, Edinburgh and London
First AMS EDITION published 1970
Manufactured in the United States of America

International Standard Book Number:
Complete Set: 0-404-5300-0
Volume 141: 0-404-53441-4

Library of Congress Catalogue Number: 72-133736

AMS PRESS INC.
NEW YORK, N.Y. 10003

The Tudor Facsimile Texts

The Two Noble Kinsmen

By "JOHN FLETCHER AND WILLIAM SHAKESPEARE"

Date of writing uncertain, probably between 1610 and 1625

Probably staged in 1626

Date of this the Earliest and only Known Edition . . 1634
[B.M. Press-mark, C. 34, g. 23]

Reproduced in Facsimile 1910

The Tudor Facsimile Texts

Under the Supervision and Editorship of

JOHN S. FARMER

The Two Noble Kinsmen

By "JOHN FLETCHER AND WILLIAM SHAKESPEARE"

1634

Issued for Subscribers by the Editor of

THE TUDOR FACSIMILE TEXTS

MCMX

The Two Noble Kinsmen

By "Mr. John Fletcher and Mr. William Shakespeare"

1634

The original of this facsimile is in the British Museum (Press-mark C. 34, g. 23).

It was first published in 1634, it is thought from a play-house copy, eighteen years after the death of Shakespeare, and nine years after Fletcher's decease. The entry in the Stationers' Books is dated April 8th, 1634.

Fletcher is by most scholars held responsible for the greater portion of the work: the part supposed to have been taken by Shakespeare has been the source of interminable criticism and contention.

The time of composition has also been the theme of much discussion. Critics are inclined to the view that "Shakespeare's part" may be set down to the period between 1610 and 1612, a Fletcher recasting to about 1622-25, and its staging to the following year (1626) at the Blackfriars Theatre.

Mr. J. A. Herbert, of the Manuscript Department of the British Museum, comparing this facsimile with the original, says :—

JOHN S. FARMER.

TWO NOBLE KINSMEN:

Presented at the Blackfriers
by the Kings Maiesties servants,
with great applause:

Written by the memorable Worthies
of their time;

Mr. *John Fletcher*, and ⎱
Mr. *William Shakspeare*. ⎰ Gent.

Printed at *London* by *Tho. Cotes*, for *Iohn Waterson*:
and are to be sold at the signe of the *Crowne*
in *Pauls* Church-yard. 1 6 3 4.

NEw Playes, and Maydenheads, are neare a kin,
Much follow'd both, for both much mony g'yn,
If they stand sound, and well : And a good Play
(Whose modest Sceanes blush on his marriage day,
And shake to loose his honour) is like hir
That after holy Tye, and first nights stir
Yet still is Modestie, and still retaines
More of the maid to sight, than Husbands paines ;
We pray our Play may be so ; For I am sure
It has a noble Breeder, and a pure,
A learned, and a Poèt never went
More famous yet twixt Po and silver Trent.
Chaucer (of all admir'd) the Story gives,
There constant to Eternity it lives ;
If we let fall the Noblenesse of this,
And the first sound this child heare, be a hisse,
How will it shake the bones of that good man,
And make him cry from under ground, O fan
From me the witles chaffe of such a wrighter (lighter
That blastes my Bayes, and my fam'd workes makes
Then Robin Hood ? This is the feare we bring ;
For to say Truth, it were an endlesse thing,
And too ambitious to aspire to him ;
Weake as we are, and almost breathlesse swim
In this deepe water. Do but you hold out
Your helping hands, and we shall take about,
And something doe to save us : You shall heare
Sceanes though below his Art, may yet appeare
Worth two houres travell. To his bones sweet sleepe :
Content to you. If this play doe not keepe,
A little dull time from us, we perceave
Our losses fall so thicke, we must needs leave.

The Tvvo Noble Kinsmen.

Actus Primus.

*Enter Hymen with a Torch burning: a Boy, in a white
Robe before singing, and strewing Flowres: After Hymen,
a Nimph, encompast in her Tresses, bearing a wheaten Garland. Then Theseus betweene two other Nimphs with
wheaten Chaplets on their heades. Then Hipolita the Bride,
lead by Theseus, and another holding a Garland over her
head (her Tresses likewise hanging.) After her Emilia holding up her Traine.*

The Song.   *Musike.*

Oses their sharpe spines being gon,
Not royall in their smels alone,
   But in their hew.
   Maiden Pinckes, of odour faint,
Dazies smel-lesse, yet most quaint
And sweet Time true.

Prim-rose first borne, child of Ver,
Merry Spring times Herbinger,
With her bels dimme.
Oxlips, in their Cradles growing,
Mary-golds, on death beds blowing,
Larkes-heeles trymme.

B

All deere natures children: sweete-
Ly sore Bride and Bridegroomes feete   Strew
Blessing their sence.   Flowers.
Not an angle of the aire,
Bird melodious, or bird faire,
Is absent hence.

The Crow, the slaundrous Cuckoe, nor
The boding Raven, nor Clough hee
Nor chattring Pie,
May on our Bridehouse pearch or sing,
Or with them any discord bring
But from it fly.

Enter 3. *Queenes in Blacke, with vailes staind, with impe-*
riall Crownes. The 1. *Queene fals downe at the foote of*
Theseus; The 2. *fals downe at the foote of Hypolita. The*
3. *before Emilia.*
 1. *Qu.* For pitties sake and true gentilities,
Heare, and respect me.
 2. *Qu.* For your Mothers sake,
And as you wish your womb may thrive with faire ones,
Heare and respect me,
 3. *Qu.* Now for the love of him whom *Iove* hath markd
The honour of your Bed, and for the sake
Of cleere virginity, be Advocate
For us, and our distresses: This good deede
Shall raze you out o'th Booke of Trespasses
All you are set downe there.
  Theseus. Sad Lady rise.
  Hypol. Stand up.
  Emil. No knees to me.
What woman I may steed that is distrest,
Does bind me to her.
  Thes. What's your request? Deliver you for all.
  1. *Qu.* We are 3. Queenes, whose Soveraignes fel before
The wrath of cruell *Creon*; who endured
The Beakes of Ravens, Tallents of the Kights,

                                               And

And pecks of Crowes, in the fowle feilds of Thebs.
He will not suffer us to burne their bones,
To urne their ashes, nor to take th' offence
Of mortall loathsomenes from the blest eye
Of holy *Phæbus*, but infects the windes
With stench of our slaine Lords. O pitty Duke,
Thou purger of the earth, draw thy feard Sword
That does good turnes to'th world; give us the Bones
Of our dead Kings, that we may Chappell them;
And of thy boundles goodnes take some note
That for our crowned heades we have no roofe,
Save this which is the Lyons, and the Beares,
And vault to every thing.

 Thef. Pray you kneele not,
I was transported with your Speech, and suffer'd
Your knees to wrong themselves; I have heard the fortunes
Of your dead Lords, which gives me such lamenting
As wakes my vengeance, and revenge for'em.
King *Capaneus*, was your Lord the day
That he should marry you, at such a season,
As now it is with me, I met your Groome,
By *Marss Altar*, you were that time faire;
Not *Iunos Mantle* fairer then your Tresses,
Nor in more bounty spread her. Your wheaten wreathe
Was then nor threashd, nor blasted; Fortune at you
Dimpled her Cheeke with smiles : *Hercules* our kinesman
(Then weaker than your eies)laide by his Club,
He tumbled downe upon his Nemean hide
And swore his sinews thawd: O greife, and time,
Fearefull consumers, you will all devoure.

 1, *Qu.* O I hope some God,
Some God hath put his mercy in your manhood
Whereto heel infuse powre, and presse you forth
Our undertaker.

 Thef. O no knees, none Widdow,
Vnto the Helmeted-Belona use them,
And pray for me your Souldier.
Troubled I am.   *turnes away.*

2. Qu. Honoured *Hypolita*
Moſt dreaded *Amazonian*, that ha'ſt ſlaine
The Sith-tuskd-Bore;that with thy Arme as ſtrong
As it is white, waſt neere to make the male
To thy Sex captive; but that this thy Lord
Borne to uphold Creation, in that honour
Firſt nature ſtilde it in, ſhrunke thee into
The bownd thou waſt ore-flowing;at once ſubduing
Thy force, and thy affection : Soldireſſe
That equally canſt poize ſterneneſſe with pitty,
Whom now I know haſt much more power on him
Then ever he had on thee, who ow'ſt his ſtrength,
And his, Love too : who is a Servant for
The Tenour of the Speech.Deere Glaſſe of Ladies
Bid him that we whom flaming war doth ſcortch,
Vnder the ſhaddow of his Sword, may coole us :
Require him he advance it ore our heades ;
Speak't in a womans key: like ſuch a woman
As any of us three; weepe ere you faile; lend us a knee;
But touch the ground for us no longer time
Then a Doves motion, when the head's pluckt off :
Tell him if he i'th blood cizd field, lay ſwolne
Showing the Sun his Teeth; grinning at the Moone
What you would doe.

  Hip. Poore Lady, ſay no more :
I had as leiſe trace this good action with you
As that whereto I am going, and never yet
Went I ſo willing, way.My Lord is taken
Hart deepe with your diſtreſſe; Let him conſider i
Ile ſpeake anon.

  3. Qu. O my petition was   *kneele to Emilia.*
Set downe in yce, which by hot greefe uncandied
Melts into drops, ſo ſorrow wanting forme
Is preſt with deeper matter.

  Emilia. Pray ſtand up,
Your greefe is written in your cheeke.

  3. Qu. O woe,
You cannot reade it there; there through my teares,

                                        Like

Like wrinckled peobles in a glasse streame
You may behold 'em (Lady, Lady, alacke)
He that will all the Treasure know o'th earth
Must know the Center too; he that will fish
For my least minnow, let him lead his line
To catch one at my heart. O pardon me.
Extremity that sharpens sundry wits
Makes me a Foole.

 Emili. Pray you say nothing, pray you,
Who cannot feele, nor see the raine being in't,
Knowes neither wet, nor dry, if that you were
The ground-peece of some Painter, I would buy you
T'instruct me gainst a Capitall greefe indeed
Such heart peirc'd demonstration; but alas
Being a naturall Sister of our Sex
Your sorrow beates so ardently upon me,
That it shall make a counter reflect gainst
My Brothers heart, and warme it to some pitty
Though it were made of stone: pray have good comfort.

 Thes. Forward to'th Temple, leave not out a Iot
O'th sacred Ceremony.

 I. *Qu.* O This Celebration
Will long last, and be more costly then,
Your Suppliants war: Remember that your Fame
Knowles in the eare, o'th world: what you doe quickly,
Is not done rashly; your first thought is more,
Then others laboured meditance: your premeditating
More then their actions: But oh Iove, your actions
Soone as they moove, as Asprayes doe the fish,
Subdue before they touch, thinke, deere *Duke* thinke
What beds our slaine Kings have.

 2. *Qu.* What greises our beds
That our deere Lords have none.

 3. *Qu.* None fit for'th dead.
Those that with Cordes, Knives, drams precipitance,
Weary of this worlds light, have to themselves
Beene deathes most horrid Agents, humaine grace
Affords them dust and shaddow.

 I: *Qu.* But our Lords

Ly blistring fore the visitating Sunne,
And were good Kings, when living.

   Thes: It is true. and I will give you comfort,
To give your dead Lords graves:
The which to doe, must make some worke with *Creon*;

   1. *Qu.* And that worke presents it selfe to'th doing:
Now twill take forme, the heates are gone to morrow.
Then, booteles toyle must recompence it selfe,
With it's owne sweat; Now he's secure,
Not dreames, we stand before your puissance
Wrinching our holy begging in our eyes
To make petition cleere.

   2. *Qu.* Now you may take him,
Drunke with his victory.

   3. *Qu.* And his Army full
Of Bread, and sloth.

   Thes. *Artesuis* that best knowest
How to draw out fit to this enterprise,
The prim'st for this proceeding, and the number
To carry such a businesse, forth and levy
Our worthiest Instruments, whilst we despatch
This grand act of our life, this daring deede
Of Fate in wedlocke.

   1. *Qu.* Dowagers, take hands
Let us be Widdowes to our woes, delay
Commends us to a famishing hope.

   All. Farewell.

   2. *Qu.* We come unseasonably: But when could greefe
Cull forth as unpanged judgement can, fit'd time
For best solicitation.

   Thes. Why good Ladies,
This is a service, whereto I am going,
Greater then any was; it more imports me
Then all the actions that I have foregone,
Or futurely can cope.

   1. *Qu.* The more proclaiming
Our suit shall be neglected, when her Armes
Able to locke *Iove* from a Synod, shall

By warranting Moone-light corslet thee, oh when
Her twyning Cherries shall their sweetnes fall
Vpon thy tastefull lips, what wilt thou thinke
Of rotten Kings or blubberd Queenes, what care
For what thou feelst not? what thou feelst being able
To make *Mars* spurne his Drom. O if thou couch
But one night with her, every howre in't will
Take hostage of thee for a hundred, and
Thou shalt remember nothing more, then what
That Banket bids thee too.

   Hip. Though much unlike
You should be so transported, as much sorry
I should be such a Suitour; yet I thinke
Did I not by th'abstayning of my joy
Which breeds a deeper longing, cure their surfeit
That craves a present medcine, I should plucke
All Ladies scandall on me. Therefore Sir
As I shall here make tryall of my prayres,
Either presuming them to have some force,
Or sentencing for ay their vigour dombe,
Prorogue this busines, we are going about, and hang
Your Sheild afore your Heart, about that necke
Which is my ffee, and which I freely lend
To doe these poore Queenes servic.

   All Queens. Oh helpe now
Our Cause cries for your knee.

   Emil. If you grant not
My Sister her petition in that force,
With that Celerity, and nature which
Shee makes it in: from henceforth ile not dare
To aske you any thing, nor be so hardy
Ever to take a Husband.

   Thes. Pray stand up.
I am entreating of my selfe to doe
That which you k'neele to have me; *Pyrithous*
Leade on the Bride; get you and pray the Gods
For successe, and returne, omit not any thing
In the pretended Celebration : Queenes

Follow your Soldier (as before) hence you
And at the banckes of Anly meete us with
The forces you can raise, where we shall finde
The moytie of a number, for a busines,
More bigger look't; since that our Theame is haste
I stamp this kisse upon thy currant lippe,
Sweete keepe it as my Token; Set you forward
For I will see you gone.   *Exeunt towards the Temple.*
Fare well my beauteous Sister: *Pyrithous*
Keepe the feast full, bate not an howre on't.

   Pirithous. Sir
Ile follow you at heeles; The Feasts solempnity
Shall want till your returne.

   Thes. Cosen I charge you
Boudge not from Athens; We shall be returning
Ere you can end this Feast; of which I pray you
Make no abatement; once more farewell all.

   1. *Qu.* Thus do'st thou still make good the tongue o'th
   2. *Qu.* And earnst a Deity equal with Mars, (world.
   3. *Qu.* If not above him, for
Thou being but mortall makest affections bend
To Godlike honours; they themselves some say
Grone under such a Mastry.

   Thes. As we are men
Thus should we doe, being sensually subdude
We loose our humane tytle; good cheere Ladies. *Florish.*
Now turne we towards your Comforts.   *Exeunt.*

     Scæna 2. *Enter Palamon, and Arcite.*

   Arcite. Deere *Palamon*, deerer in love then Blood
And our prime Cosen, yet unhardned in
The Crimes of nature; Let us leave the Citty
Thebs, and the temptings in't, before we further
Sully our glosse of youth,
And here to keepe in abstinence we shame
As in Incontinence; for not to swim
I'th aide o'th Current, were almost to sincke,

                              At

At least to fruſtrate ſtriving, and to follow
The common Streame, t'wold bring us to an Edy
Where we ſhould turne or drowne; if labeur through,
Our gaine but life, and weakenes.

   Pal. Your advice
Is cride up with example: what ſtrange ruins
Since firſt we went to Schoole, may we perceive
Walking in Thebs? Skars, and bare weedes
The gaine o'th Martialiſt, who did propound
To his bold ends, honour, and golden Ingots,
Which though he won, he had not, and now flurted
By peace for whom he fought, who then ſhall offer
To *Marſis* ſo ſcornd *Altar?* I doe bleede
When ſuch I meete, and wiſh great *Iuno* would
Reſume her ancient fit of *Ielouzie*
To get the Soldier worke, that peace might purge
For her repletion, and retaine anew
Her charitable heart now hard, and harſher
Then ſtrife, or war could be.

   Arcite, Are you not out?
Meete you no ruine, but the Soldier in
The Cranckes, and turnes of Thebs? you did begin
As if you met decaies of many kindes:
Perceive you none, that doe arowſe your pitty
But th'un-conſiderd Seldier?

   Paj. Yes, I pitty
Decaies where e'er I finde them, but ſuch moſt
That ſweating in an honourable Toyle
Are paide with yce to coole 'em.

   Arcite, Tis not this
I did begin to ſpeake of: This is vertue
Of no reſpect in Thebs, I ſpake of Thebs
How dangerous if we will keepe our Honours,
It is for our reſyding, where every evill
Hath a good cullor; where eve'ry ſeeming good's
A certaine evill, where not to be ev'n lumpe
As they are, here were to be ſtrangers, and
Such things to be meere Monſters.

C

Pal. Tis in our power,
(Vnleſſe we feare that Apes can Tutor's)to
Be Maſters of our manners : what neede I
Affect anothers gate, which is not catching
Where there is faith, or to be fond upon
Anothers way of ſpeech, when by mine owne
I may be reaſonably conceiv'd ; ſav'd too,
Speaking it truly ; why am I bound
By any generous bond to follow him
Followes his Taylor, haply ſo long untill
The follow'd, make purſuit ? or let me know,
Why mine owne Barber is unbleſt, with him
My poore Chinne too, for tis not Cizard iuſt
To ſuch a Favorites glaſſe : What Cannon is there
That does command my Rapier from my hip
To dangle't in my hand, or to go tip toe
Before the ſtreete be foule ? Either I am
The fore-horſe in the Teame, or I am none
That draw i'th ſequent trace : theſe poore ſleight ſores,
Neede not a plantin ; That which rips my boſome
Almoſt to'th heart's,
   Arcite. Our Vncle *Creon.*
   Pal. He,
A moſt unbounded Tyrant, whoſe ſucceſſes
Makes heaven unfeard, and villany aſſured
Beyond its power : there's nothing, almoſt puts
Faith in a feavour, and deifies alone
Voluble chance, who onely attributes
The faculties of other Inſtruments
To his owne Nerves and act ; Commands men ſervice,
And what they winne in't, boot and glory on;
That feares not to do harm ; good, dares not ; Let
The blood of mine that's ſibbe to him, be ſuckt
From me with Leeches, Let them breake and fall
Off me with that corruption.
   Arc. Cleere ſpirited Cozen
Lets leave his Court, that we may nothing ſhare,
Of his lowd infamy : for our milke,

Will

Will relifh of the pafture, and we muft
Be vile, or difobedient, not his kinefmen
In blood, unleffe in quality.

   Pal. Nothing truer:
I thinke the Ecchoes of his fhames have dea'ft
The eares of heav'nly Iuftice: widdows cryes
Defcend againe into their throates, and have not: *Enter Va-*
Due audience of the Gods: *Valerius*   *(lerius.*

   Val. The King cals for you; yet be leaden footed
Till his great rage be off him. *Phebus* when
He broke his whipftocke and exclaimd against
The Horfes of the Sun, but whisperd too
The lowdeneffe of his Fury.

   Pal. Small windes fhake him,
But whats the matter?

   Val. Thefeus (who where he threates appals,) hath fent
Deadly defyance to him, and pronounces
Ruine to Thebs, who is at hand to feale
The promife of his wrath.

   Arc. Let him approach;
But that we feare the Gods in him, he brings not
A jot of terrour to us; Yet what man
Thirds his owne worth (the cafe is each of ours)
When that his actions dregd, with minde affurd
Tis bad he goes about.

   Pal. Leave that unreafond.
Our fervices ftand now for Thebs, not *Creon,*
Yet to be neutrall to him, were difhonour;
Rebellious to oppofe: therefore we muft
With him ftand to the mercy of our Fate,
Who hath bounded our laft minute.

   Arc. So we muft;
Ift fed this warres afoote? or it fhall be
On faile of fome condition.

   Val. Tis in motion
The intelligence of ftate came in the inftant
With the defier.

Pal. Lets to the king, who, were he
A quarter carrier of that honour, which
His Enemy come in, the blood we venture
Should be as for our health, which were not spent,
Rather laide out for purchase: but alas
Our hands advanc'd before our hearts, what will
The fall o'th stroke doe damage?

Arci. Let th'event,
That never erring Arbitratour, tell us
When we know all our selves, and let us follow
The becking of our chance.　　　　　*Exeunt.*

Scæna 3. *Enter Pirithous, Hipolita, Emilia.*

Pir. No further.

Hip. Sir farewell; repeat my wishes
To our great Lord, of whose succes I dare not
Make any timerous question, yet I wish him
Exces, and overflow of power, and't might be
To dare ill-dealing fortune; speede to him,
Store never hurtes good Gouernours.

Pir. Though I know
His Ocean needes not my poore drops, yet they
Must yeild their tribute there: My precious Maide,
Those best affections, that the heavens infuse
In their best temper'd peices, keepe enthroand
In your deare heart.

Emil. Thanckes Sir; Remember me
To our all royall Brother, for whose speede
The great Bellona ile soilicite; and
Since in our terrene State petitions are not
Without giftes understood: Ile offer to her
What I shall be advised she likes; our hearts
Are in his Army in his Tent.

Hip. In's bosome:
We have bin Soldiers, and wee cannot weepe
When our Friends don their helmes, or put to sea,
Or tell of Babes broachd on the Launce, or women

That

That have fod their Infants in (and after eate them)
The brine, they wept at killing 'em; Then if
You ſtay to ſee of us ſuch Spincſters, we
Should hold you here for e ver.

   Pir. Peace be to you
As I purſue this war, which shall be then
Beyond further requiring.   *Exit Pir.*

   Emil. How his longing
Followes his Friend; ſince his depart, his ſportes
Though craving ſeriouſnes, and skilll, paſt ſlightly
His careles execution, where nor gaine
Made him regard, or loſſe conſider, but
Playing ore buſines in his hand, another
Directing in his head, his minde, nurſe equall
To theſe ſo diffring Twyns; have you obſerv'd him,
Since our great Lord departed?

   Hip. With much labour :
And I did love him ſort, they two have Cabind
In many as dangerous, as poore a Corner,
Perill and want contending, they have skift
Torrents whoſe roring' tyranny and power
I'thleaſt of theſe was dreadfull, and they have
Fought out together, where Deaths-ſelſe was lodgd,
Yet fate hath brought them off : Their knot of love
Tide, weau'd, intangled, with ſo true, ſo long,
And with a finger of ſo deepe a cunning
May be outworne, never undone. I thinke
Theſeu cannot be umpire to himſelfe
Cleaving his conſcience into twaine, and doing
Each ſide like Iuſtice, which he loves beſt.

   Emil. Doubtleſſe
There is a beſt, and reaſon has no manners
To ſay it is not you; I was acquainted
Once with a time, when I enjoyd a Play-fellow;
You were at wars, when she the grave enrichd,
Who made too proud the Bed, tooke leave o'th Moone
(which then lookt pale at parting) when our count
Was each a eleven.

Hip. Twas *Flauia.*

Emil. Yes

You talke of *Pirithous* and *Theseus* love;
Theirs has more ground, is more maturely seafond,
More buckled with strong Iudgement. and their needes
The one of th'other may be faid to water
Their intertangled rootes of love, but I
And fhee (I figh and fpoke of) were things innocent,
Lou'd for we did, and like the Elements
That know not what, nor why, yet doe effect
Rare iffues by their operance; our foules
Did fo to one another; what fhe lik'd,
Was then of me approov'd, what not condemd
No more arraignement, the flowre that I would plucke
And put betweene my breafts, oh(then but beginning
To fwell about the bloffome)fhe would long
Till fhee had fuch another, and commit it
To the like innocent Cradle, where *Phenix* like
They dide in perfume: on my head no toy
But was her patterne, her affections (pretty
Though happely, her careles, were, I followed
For my moft ferious decking, had mine eare
Stolne fome new aire, or at adventure humd on
From muficall Coynadge; why it was a note
Whereon her fpirits would fojourne (rather dwell on)
And fing it in her flumbers; This rehearfall
(Which fury-innocent wots weil)comes in
Like old importments baftard, has this end,
That the true love tweene Mayde, and mayde, may be
More then in fex individuall.

   Hip. Y'are ont of breath
And this high fpeeded-pace, is but to fay
That you fhall never (like the Maide *Flauina*)
Love any that's calld Man.

   Emil. I am fure I fhall not.

   Hip. Now alacke weake Sifter,
I muft no more beleeve thee in this point
(Though, in't I know thou doft beleeve thy felfe,)

2. Hearfes rea-
dy with Pala-
mon; and Arci-
te: the 3.
Queenes.
Thefeus : and
his Lordes
ready.

                                           Then

Then I will truſt a ſickely appetite,
That loathes even as it longs, but ſure my Siſter
If I were ripe for your perſwaſion, you
Have ſaide enough to ſhake me from the Arme
Of the all noble *Theſeus*, for whoſe fortunes,
I will now in, and kneele with great aſſurance,
That we, more then his *Pirothous*, poſſeſſe
The high throne in his heart.

 Emil. I am not againſt your faith,
Yet I continew mine.   *Exeunt.*
            Cornets.

*Scæna 4. A Battaile ſtrooke with him: Then a Retrait: Floriſh.
Then Enter Theſeus (victor) the three Queenes meete
him, and fall on their faces before him.*

 1. *Qu.* To thee no ſtarre be darke.
 2. *Qu.* Both heaven and earth
Friend thee for ever.
 3. *Qu.* All the good that may
Be wiſhd upon thy head, I cry Amen too't.   (vens
 Theſ. Th'imparciall Gods, who from the mounted hea-
View us their mortall Heard, behold who erre,
And in their time chaſtice: goe and finde out
The bones of your dead Lords, and honour them
With treble Ceremonie, rather then a gap
Should be in their deere rights, we would ſuppl'it.
But thoſe we will depute, which ſhall inveſt
You in your dignities, and even each thing
Our haſt does leave imperfect; So adiew
And heavens good eyes looke on you. what are thoſe?
           Exeunt Queenes.
 Herald. Men of great quality, as may be judgd
By their appointment; Some of Thebs have told's
They are Siſters children, Nephewes to the King.
 Theſ. By'th Helme of Mars, I ſaw them in the war,
Like to a paire of Lions, ſmeard with prey,
Make lanes in troopes agaſt. I fixt my note
Conſtantly on them; for they were a marke

            Worth

Worth a god's view: what prisoner was't that told me
When I enquired their names?

    Herald. We leave, they'r called
Arcite and *Palamon,*

    Thes. Tis right, those, those
They are not dead?

    Her. Nor in a state of life, had they bin taken
When their last hurts were given, twas possible
They might have bin recovered; Yet they breathe
And haue the name of men.

    Thes. Then like men use 'em
The very lees of such (millions of rates)
Exceede the wine of others: all our Surgions
Convent in their behoofe, our richest balmes
Rather then niggard wast, their lives concerne us,
Much more then Thebs is worth, rather then have 'em
Freed of this plight, and in their morning state
(Sound and at liberty) I would 'em dead,
But forty thousand fold, we had rather have 'em
Prisoners to us, then death; Beare 'em speedily
From our kinde aire, to them unkinde, and minister
What man to man may doe for our sake more,
Since I have knowne frights, fury, friends, beheastes,
Loves, provocations, zeale, a mistris Taske,
Desire of liberty, a feavour, madnes,
Hath set a marke which nature could not reach too
Without some imposition, sicknes in will
Or wrastling strength in reason, for our Love
And great *Appollos* mercy, all our best,
Their best skill tender. Leade into the Citty,
Where having bound things scatterd, we will post *Florish.*
To Athens for our Army.   *Exeunt.*
                                Musicke.

    *Scæna 5. Enter the Queenes with the Hearses of their
Knightes, in a Funerall Solempnity, &c.*

*Vrnes and odours, bring away,
Vapours, sighes, darken the day ;*

                                      Our

3.Hearses rea-
dy.

Our dole more deadly lookes than dying
Balmes, and Gummes, and heavy cheeres,
Sacred vials fill'd with teares,
And clamors through the wild ayre flying.

Come all sad, and solempne Showes,
That are quick-eyd pleasures foes;
We convent nought else but woes.   *We convent, &c.*

3. *Qu.* This funeral path, brings to your housholds grave:
Ioy ceaze on you againe: peace sleepe with him.
   2. *Qu.* And this to yours.
   1. *Qu.* Yours this way: Heavens lend
A thousand differing waies, to one sure end.
   3. *Qu.* This world's a Citty full of straying Streetes,
And Death's the market place, where each one meetes.
                                    Exeunt severally.

Actus Secundus.

Scæna 1. *Enter Iailor, and Wooer.*

Iailor. I may depart with little, while I live, some thing I
May cast to you, not much: Alas the Prison I
Keepe, though it be for great ones, yet they seldome
Come; Before one *Salmon*, you shall take a number
Of Minnowes: I am given out to be better lyn'd
Then it can appeare, to me report is a true
Speaker: I would I were really, that I am
Deliverd to be: Marry, what I have (be it what
it will) I will assure upon my daughter at
The day of my death.
   Wooer. Sir I demaund no more then your owne offer,
And I will estate your Daughter in what I
Have promised,

                    D   *Iailor.*

*Iailor.*Wel,we will talke more of this,when the solemnity
Is past ; But have you a full promise of her?

Enter Daughter.

When that shall be seene,I tender my consent.

Wooer. I have Sir; here shee comes.

Iailor. Your Friend and I have chanced to name
You here,upon the old busines: But no more of that.
Now,so soone as the Court hurry is over,we will
Have an end of it:I'th meane time looke tenderly
To the two Prisoners. I can tell you they are princes.

*Daug.*These strewings are for their Chamber;tis pitty they
Are in prison, and twer pitty they should be out : I
Doe thinke they have patience to make any adversity
Asham'd ; the prison it selfe is proud of 'em; and
They have all the world in their Chamber.

Iailor. They are fam'd to be a paire of absolute men.

*Daugh.*By my troth,I think Fame but stammers 'em,they
Stand a greise above the reach of report.   (doers.

Iai. I heard them reported in the Battaile, to be the only

Daugh. Nay most likely,for they are noble suffrers;I
Mervaile how they would have lookd had they beene
Victors, that with such a constant Nobility,enforce
A freedome out of Bondage, making misery their
Mirth,and affliction, a toy to jest at.

Iailor. Doe they so?

Daug. It seemes to me they have no more sence of their
Captivity, then I of ruling Athens : they eate
Well, looke merrily, discourse of many things,
But nothing of their owne restraint, and disasters :
Yet sometime a devided sigh,martyrd as twer
I'th deliverance, will breake from one of them.
When the other presently gives it so sweete a rebuke,
That I could wish my selfe a Sigh to be so chid,
Or at least a Sigher to be comforted.

Wooer. I never saw'em.

Iailor. The Duke himselfe came privately in the night,

Enter Palamon, and Arcite, above.

And so did they, what the reason of it is, I

Know

Know not: Looke yonder they are; that's
Arcite lookes out.

Daugh. No Sir, no, that's *Palamon* : *Arcite* is the
Lower of the twaine ; you may perceive a part
Of him.

Iai. Goe too, leave your pointing ; they would not
Make us their object; out of their sight.

Daugh. It is a holliday to looke on them: Lord, the
Diffrence of men. *Exeunt.*

Scæna 2. *Enter Palamon, and Arcite in prison.*

Pal. How doe you Noble Cosen ?

Arcite. How doe you Sir ?

Pal. Why strong inough to laugh at misery,
And beare the chance of warre yet, we are prisoners
I feare for ever Cosen.

Arcite. I beleeve it,
And to that destiny have patiently
Laide up my houre to come.

Pal. Oh Cosen *Arcite,*
Where is Thebs now ? where is our noble Country ?
Where are our friends, and kindreds ? never more
Must we behold those comforts, never see
The hardy youthes strive for the Games of honour
(Hung with the painted favours of their Ladies)
Like tall Ships under saile: then start among'st 'em
And as an Eastwind leave 'em all behinde us,
Like lazy Clowdes, whilst *Palamon* and *Arcite,*
Even in the wagging of a wanton leg
Out-stript the peoples praises, won the Garlands,
Ere they have time to wish 'em ours. O never
Shall we two exercise, like Twyns of honour,
Our Armes againe, and feele our fyry horses
Like proud Seas under us, our good Swords, now
(Better the red-eyd god of war nev'r were)
Bravishd our sides, like age must run to rust,
And decke the Temples of those gods that hate us,

D 2 These

These hands shall never draw'em out like lightning
To blast whole Armies more.

  Arcite. No *Palamon*,
Those hopes are Prisoners with us, here we are
And here the graces of our youthes must wither
Like a too-timely Spring; here age must finde us,
And which is heaviest (*Palamon*) unmarried,
The sweete embraces of a loving wife
Loden with kisses, armd with thousand Cupids
Shall never claspe our neckes, no issue know us,
No figures of our selves shall we ev'r see,
To glad our age, and like young Eagles teach'em
Boldly to gaze against bright armes, and say
Remember what your fathers were, and conquer.
The faire-eyd Maides, shall weepe our Banishments,
And in their Songs, curse ever-blinded fortune
Till shee for shame see what a wrong she has done
To youth and nature; This is all our world;
We shall know nothing here but one another,
Heare nothing but the Clocke that tels our woes.
The Vine shall grow, but we shall never see it:
Sommer shall come, and with her all delights;
But dead-cold winter must inhabite here still.

  Pal. Tis too true *Arcite.* To our Theban houndes,
That shooke the aged Forrest with their ecchoes,
No more now must we halloa, no more shake
Our pointed Iavelyns, whilst the angry Swine
Flyes like a parthian quiver from our rages,
Strucke with our well-steeld Darts: All valiant uses,
(The foode, and nourishment of noble mindes,)
In us two here shall perish; we shall die
(which is the curse of honour) lastly,
Children of greife, and Ignorance.

  Arc. Yet Cosen,
Even from the bottom of these miseries
From all that fortune can inflict upon us,
I see two comforts ryfing, two meere blessings,
If the gods please, to hold here a brave patience,

And the enjoying of our greefes together:
Whilst *Palamon* is with me, let me perish
If I thinke this our prison.

Pala. Certeinly,
Tis a maine goodnes Cosen, that our fortunes
Were twyn'd together; tis most true, two soules
Put in two noble Bodies, let'em suffer
The gaule of hazard, so they grow together,
Will never sincke, they must not, say they could,
A willing man dies sleeping, and all's done.

Arc. Shall we make worthy uses of this place
That all men hate so much?

Pal. How gentle Cosen!

Arc. Let's thinke this prison, holy sanctuary,
To keepe us from corruption of worse men,
We are young and yet desire the waies of honour,
That liberty and common Conversation
The poyson of pure spirits; might like women
Wooe us to wander from. What worthy blessing
Can be but our Imaginations
May make it ours? And heere being thus together,
We are an endles mine to one another;
We are one anothers wife, ever begetting
New birthes of love; we are father, friends, acquaintance,
We are in one another, Families,
I am your heire, and you are mine: This place
Is our Inheritance: no hard Oppressour
Dare take this from us; here with a little patience
We shall live long, and loving: No surfeits seeke us:
The hand of war hurts none here, nor the Seas
Swallow their youth: were we at liberty,
A wife might part us lawfully, or busines,
Quarrels consume us, Envy of ill men
Crave our acquaintance, I might sicken Cosen,
Where you should never know it, and so perish
Without your noble hand to close mine eies,
Or praiers to the gods; a thousand chaunces
Were we from hence, would seaver us.

Pal.

Pal. You have made me
(I thanke you Cosen *Arcite*)almost wanton
With my Captivity: what a misery
It is to live abroade? and every where:
Tis like a Beast me thinkes: I finde the Court here,
I am sure a more content, and all those pleasures
That wooe the wils of men to vanity,
I see through now, and am sufficient
To tell the world,tis but a gaudy shaddow,
That old Time,as he passes by takes with him,
What had we bin old in the Court of *Creon,*
Where sin is Iustice, lust, and ignorance,
The vertues of the great ones:Cosen *Arcite,*
Had not the loving gods found this place for us
We had died as they doe,ill old men,unwept,
And had their Epitaphes,the peoples Curses,
Shall I say more?

   Arc. I would heare you still.

   Pal. Ye shall.
Is there record of any two that lov'd
Better then we doe *Arcite?*

   Arc. Sure there cannot.

   Pal. I doe not thinke it possible our friendship
Should ever leave us.

   Arc. Till our deathes it cannot

                              Enter Emilia and her woman.
And after death our spirits shall be led
To those that love eternally. Speake on Sir.
This garden has a world of pleasures in't.

   Emil. What Flowre is this?

   Wom. Tis calld Narcissus Madam.

   Emil. That was a faire Boy certaine, but a foole,
To love himselfe, were there not maides enough?

   Arc. Pray forward.

   Pal. Yes.

   Emil. Or were they all hard hearted?

   Wom. They could not be to one so faire.

   Emil. Thou wouldst not.

                                              Wom.

Wom. I thinke I should not, Madam.

Emil. That's a good wench:

But take heede to your kindnes though.

Wom. Why Madam?

Emil. Men are mad things.

Arcite. Will ye goe forward Cosen?

Emil. Canst not thou work: such flowers in silke wench?

Wom. Yes.

Emil. Ile have a gowne full of 'em and of these,

This is a pretty colour, wilt not doe

Rarely upon a Skirt wench?

Wom. Deinty Madam.

Arc. Cosen, Cosen, how doe you Sir? Why *Palamon?*

Pal. Never till now I was in prison *Arcite.*

Arc. Why whats the matter Man?

Pal. Behold, and wonder.

By heaven shee is a Goddesse.

Arcite. Ha.

Pal. Doe reverence.

She is a Goddesse *Arcite.*

Emil. Of all Flowres,

Me thinkes a Rose is best.

Wom. Why gentle Madam?

Emil. It is the very Embleme of a Maide.

For when the west wind courts her gently

How modestly she blowes, and paints the Sun,

With her chaste blushes? When the North comes neere her,

Rude and impatient, then, like Chastity

Shee lockes her beauties in her bud againe,

And leaves him to base briers.

Wom. Yet good Madam,

Sometimes her modesty will blow so far

She fals for't: a Mayde

If shee have any honour, would be loth

To take example by her.

Emil. Thou art wanton.

Arc. She is wondrous faire.

Pal. She is all the beauty extant.

Emil.

Emil. The Sun grows high, lets walk in, keep thefe flowers,
Weele fee how neere Art can come neere their colours;
I am wondrous merry hearted, I could laugh now.

Wom. I could lie downe I am fure.

Emil. And take one with you?

Wom. That's as we bargaine Madam,

Emil. Well, agree then.

                              Exeunt Emilia and woman.

Pal. What thinke you of this beauty?

Arc. Tis a rare one.

Pal. Is't but a rare one?

Arc. Yes a matchles beauty.

Pal. Might not a man well lofe himfelfe and loye her?

Arc. I cannot tell what you have done, I have,
Befhrew mine eyes for't, now I feele my Shackles.

Pal. You love her then?

Arc. Who would not?

Pal. And defire her?

Arc. Before my liberty.

Pal. I faw her firft.

Arc. That's nothing

Pal. But it fhall be.

Arc. I faw her too.

Pal. Yes, but you muft not love her.

Arc. I will not as you doe; to worfhip her;
As fhe is heavenly, and a bleffed Goddes,
(I love her as a woman, to enjoy her)
So both may love.

Pal. You fhall not love at all.

Arc. Not love at all.
Who fhall deny me?

Pal. I that firft faw her; I that tooke poffeffion
Firft with mine eye of all thofe beauties
In her reveald to mankinde: if thou lou'ft her.
Or entertain'ft a hope to blaft my wifhes,
Thou art a Traytour *Arcite* and a fellow
Falfe as thy Title to her: friendfhip, blood
And all the tyes betweene us I difclaime

                                                    If

If thou once thinke upon her.

 Arc, Yes I love her,
And if the lives of all my name lay on it,
I muſt doe ſo, I love her with my ſoule,
If that will loſe ye, farewell *Palamon,*
I ſay againe, I love, and in loving her maintaine
I am as worthy, and as free a lover
And have as juſt a title to her beauty
As any *Palamon* or any living
That is a mans Sonne.

 Pal. Have I cald thee friend?

 Arc. Yes, and have found me ſo; why are you mov'd thus?
Let me deale coldly with you, am not I
Part of your blood, part of your ſoule? you have told me
That I was *Palamon,* and you were *Arcite.*

 Pal. Yes.

 Arc, Am not I liable to thoſe affections,
Thoſe joyes, greifes, angers, feares, my friend ſhall ſuffer?

 Pal. Ye may be.

 Arc. Why then would you deale ſo cunningly,
So ſtrangely, ſo vnlike a noble kineſman
To love alone? ſpeake truely, doe you thinke me
Vnworthy of her ſight?

 Pal. No; but unjuſt,
If thou purſue that ſight.

 Arc. Becauſe an other
Firſt ſees the Enemy, ſhall I ſtand ſtill
And let mine honour downe, and never charge?

 Pal. Yes, if he be but one.

 Arc. But ſay that one
Had rather combat me?

 Pal. Let that one ſay ſo,
And uſe thy freedome: els if thou purſueſt her,
Be as that curſed man that hates his Country,
A branded villaine.

 Arc. You are mad.

 Pal. I muſt be.
Till thou art worthy, *Arcite,* it concernes me,

    E   And

And in this madnes,if I hazard thee
And take thy life, I deale but truely.
  Arc. Fie Sir.
You play the Childe extreamely:I will love her,
I muſt, I ought to dee ſo,and I dare,
And all this juſtly.
  Pal. O that now,that now
Thy falſe-ſelfe and thy friend, had but this fortune
To be one howre at liberty, and graſpe
Our good Swords in our hands,I would quickly teach thee
What tw'er to filch affection from another :
Thou art baſer in it then a Cutpurſe;
Put but thy head out of this window more,
And as I have a ſoule, Ile naile thy life too't.
  Arc. Thou dar'ſt not foole,thou canſt not,thou art feeble.
Put my head out?Ile throw my Body out,
And leape the garden, when I ſee her next
                              Enter Keeper.
And pitch between her armes to anger thee.
  Pal. No more;the keeper's comming; I ſhall live
To knocke thy braines out with my Shackles.
  Arc. Doe.
  Keeper. By your leave Gentlemen;
  Pala. Now honeſt keeper ?
  Keeper. Lord *Arcite*,you muſt preſently to'th Duke;
The cauſe I know not yet.
  Arc. I am ready keeper.
  Keeper. Prince *Palamon*,I muſt awhile bereave you
Of your faire Coſens Company.
                    Exeunt Arcite, and Keeper.
  Pal. And me too,
Even when you pleaſe of life;why is he ſent for?
It may be he ſhall marry her,he's goodly,
And like enough the Duke hath taken notice
Both of his blood and body:But his falſehood,
Why ſhould a friend be treacherous ? If that
Get him a wife ſo noble, and ſo faire;
Let honeſt men ne're love againe. Once more

I

I would but see this faire One: Bleſſed Gar len,
And fruite, and flowers more bleſſed that ſtill bloſſom
As her brighr eies ſhine on ye, would I were
For all the fortune of my life hereafter
Yon little Tree, yon bloowing Apricocke;
How I would ſpread, and fling my wanton armes
In at her window; I would bring her fruite
Fit for the Gods to feed on: youth and pleaſure
Still as ſhe taſted ſhould be doubled on her,
And if ſhe be not heavenly I would make her
So neere the Gods in nature, they ſhould feare her.

Enter Keeper.

And then I am ſure ſhe would love me: how now keeper
Wher's *Arcite,*

Keeper, Baniſhd: Prince *Pirithous*
Obtained his libe ty; but never more
Vpon his oth and life muſt he ſet foote
Vpon this Kingdome.

Pal. Hees a bleſſed man,
He ſhall ſee Thebs againe, and call to Armes
The bold yong men, that when he bids 'em charge,
Fall on like fire: *Arcite* ſhall have a Fortune,
If he dare make himſelfe a worthy Lover,
Yet in the Feild to ſtrike a battle for her;
And if he loſe her then, he's a cold Coward;
How bravely may he beare himſelfe to win her
If he be noble *Arcite*; thouſand waies.
Were I at liberty, I would doe things
Of ſuch a vertuous greatnes, that this Lady,
This bluſhing virgine ſhould take manhood to her
And ſeeke to raviſh me.

Keeper, My Lord for you
I have this charge too.

Pal. To diſcharge my life.

Keep. No, but from this place to remoove your Lordſhip,
The windowes are too open.

Pal. Devils take 'em
That are ſo envious to me; pre'thee kill me.

Keeper

Keep. And hang for't afterward.

Pal. By this good light
Had I a sword I would kill thee.

Keep, Why my Lord?

Pal. Thou bringst such pelting scuruy news continually
Thou art not worthy life; I will not goe.

Keep. Indeede yon must my Lord.

Pal. May I see the garden?

Keep. Noe.

Pal. Then I am resolud, I will not goe.   (rous

Keep. I must constraine you then ; and for you are dange-
Ile clap more yrons on you.

Pal. Doe good keeper.
Ile shake 'em so, ye shall not sleepe,
Ile make ye a new Morrisse, must I goe ?

Keep. There is no remedy.

Pal. Farewell kinde window.
May rude winde never hurt thee. O my Lady
If ever thou hast felt what sorrow was,
Dreame how I suffer. Come; now bury me.

Exeunt Palamon, and Keeper.
Scæna 3. *Enter Arcite.*

Arcite. Banishd the kingdome? tis a benefit,
A mercy I must thanke 'em for, but banishd
The free enjoying of that face I die for,
Oh twas a studdied punishment, a death
Beyond Imagination: Such a vengeance
That were I old and wicked, all my sins
Could never plucke upon me, *Palamon*;
Thou ha'st the Start now, thou shalt stay andsee
Her bright eyes breake each morning gainst thy window,
And let in life into thee ; thou shalt feede
Vpon the sweetenes of a noble beauty,
That nature nev'r exceeded, nor nev'r shall:
Good gods ? what happines has *Palamon*?
Twenty to one, hee'le come to speake to her,
And if she be as gentle, as she's faire,

I know she's his, he has a Tongue will tame   (can come)
Tempests, and make the wild Rockes wanton. Come what
The worst is death; I will not leave the Kingdome,
I know mine owne, is but a heape of ruins,
And no redresse there, if I goe, he has her.
I am resolu'd an other shape shall make me,
Or end my fortunes. Either way, I am happy:
Ile see her, and be neere her, or no more.

Enter. 4. Country people, & one with a Garlou before them.

  1, My Masters, ile be there that's certaine.
  2. And Ile be there.
  3. And I.
  4. Why then have with ye Boyes; Tis but a chiding,
Let the plough play to day, ile tick'It out
Of the lades tailes to morrow.
   1. I am sure
To have my wife as jealous as a Turkey:
But that's all one, ile goe through, let her mumble.
  2. Clap her aboard to morrow night, and stoa her,
And all's made up againe.
  3. I, doe but put a feskue in her fist, and you shall see her
Take a new lesson out, and be a good wench.
Doe we all hold, against the Maying?
  4. Hold? what should aile us?
  3. *Arcas* will be there.
  2. And *Sennois.*
And *Rycas,* and 3. better lads nev'r dancd under green Tree,
And yet know what wenches: ha?
But will the dainty Domine the Schoolemaster keep touch
Doe you thinke: for he do's all ye know.
  3. Hee'l eate a hornebooke ere he faile: goe too, the matter's too farre driven betweene him, and the Tanners daughter, to let slip now, and she must see the Duke, and she must
daunce too.
  4. Shall we be lusty.
  2. All the Boyes in Athens blow wind i'th breech on's,
                E 3   and

and heere ile be and there ile be, for our Towne, and here
againe, and there againe : ha, Boyes, heigh for the wea-
vers.

  1. This muſt be done i'th woods.

  4. O pardon me.

  2. By any meanes our thing of learning ſees ſo : where he
himſelfe will edifie the Duke moſt parlouſly in our behalſes:
hees excellent i'th woods, bring him to'th plaines, his learning makes no cry.

  3. Weele ſee the ſports, then every man to's Tackle: and
Sweete Companions lets rehearſe by any meanes before
The Ladies ſee us, and doe ſweetly, and God knows what
May come on't.

  4. Content; the ſports once ended, wee'l performe. Away
Boyes and hold.

  Arc. By your leaves honeſt friends : pray you whither
goe you.

  4. Whither ? why, what a queſtion's that ?

  Arc. Yes, tis a queſtion, to me that know not.

  3. To the *Game* my Friend.

  2. Where were you bred you know it not ?

  Arc. Not farre Sir,
Are there ſuch *Games* to day ?

  1. Yes marry are there :
And ſuch as you neuer ſaw ; The *Duke* himſelfe
Will be in perſon there.

  Arc. What paſtimes are they ?

  2. Wraſtling, and Running ; Tis a pretty Fellow.

  3. Thou wilt not goe along.

  Arc. Not yet Sir.

  4. Well Sir
Take your owne time, come Boyes

  1. My minde miſgives me
This fellow has a veng'ance tricke o'th hip,
Marke how his Bodi's made for't

  2. Ile be hangd though
If he dare venture, hang him plumb porredge,
He wraſtle? he roſt eggs. Come lets be gon Lads. *Exeunt* 4.
                                              Arc.

Arc. This is an offerd oportunity
I durst not wish for. Well, I could have wrestled,
The best men call'd it excellent, and run
Swifter, then winde upon a feild of Corne
(Curling the wealthy eares) never flew: Ile venture,
And in some poore disguize be there, who knowes
Whether my browes may not be girt with garlands?
And happines preferre me to a place,
Where I may ever dwell in sight of her.   *Exit Arcite,*

Scæna 4. *Enter Iailors Daughter alone.*

Daugh. Why should I love this Gentleman? Tis odds
He never will affect me; I am base,
My Father the meane Keeper of his Prison,
And he a prince; To marry him is hopelesse;
To be his whore, is witles; Out upon't;
What pushes are we wenches driven to
When fifteene once has found us? First I saw him,
I (seeing) thought he was a goodly man;
He has as much to please a woman in him,
(If he please to bestow it so) as ever
These eyes yet lookt on; Next, I pittied him,
And so would any young wench o' my Conscience
That ever dream'd, or vow'd her Maydenhead
To a yong hansom Man; Then I lov'd him,
(Extreamely lov'd him) infinitely lov'd him;
And yet he had a Cosen, faire as he too.
But in my heart was *Palamon,* and there
Lord, what a coyle he keepes? To heare him
Sing in an evening, what a heaven it is?
And yet his Songs are sad-ones; Fairer spoken,
Was never Gentleman. When I come in
To bring him water in a morning, first
He bowes his noble body, then salutes me, thus:
Faire, gentle Mayde, good morrow, may thy goodnes,
Get thee a happy husband; Once he kist me,
I lov'd my lips the better ten daies after,
Would he would doe so ev'ry day; He greives much,
And me as much to see his misery.

What

What fhould I doe,to make him know I love him,
For I would faine enjoy him? Say I ventur'd
To fet him free? what faies the law then? Thus much
For Law,or kindred: I will doe it,
And this night,or to morrow he fhall love me.   *Exit.*

Scæna 4. *Enter Thefeus, Hipolita, Pirithous,*
Emilia : Arcite with a Garland, &c.

This fhort flo-
rifh of Cor-
nets and
Showtes with-
in.

Thef: You have done worthily; I have not feene
Since *Hercules*,a man of tougher fynewes;
What ere you are,you run the beft,and wraftle,
That thefe times can allow.

Arcite. I am proud to pleafe you,

Thef. What Countrie bred you?

Arcite. This; but far off,Prince.

Thef. Are you a Gentleman?

Arcite. My father faid fo;
And to thofe gentle ufes gave me life.

Thef. Are you his heire?

Arcite. His yongeft Sir.

Thef. Your Father
Sure is a happy Sire then : what prooves you?

Arcite. A little of all noble Quallities :
I could have kept a Hawke,and well have holloa'd
To a deepe crie of Dogges; I dare not praife
My feat in horfemanfhip : yet they that knew me
Would fay it was my beft peece : laft,and greateft,
I would be thought a Souldier.

Thef. You are perfect.

Pirith. Vpon my foule,a proper man.

Emilia. He is fo.

Per. How doe you like him Ladie?

Hip. I admire him,
I have not feene fo yong a man,fo noble
(If he fay true,)of his fort.

Emil. Beleeve,
His mother was a wondrous handfome woman,
His face me thinkes,goes that way.

Hyp. But his Body

And

And firie minde, illuſtrate a brave Father.

Per. Marke how his vertue, like a hidden Sun
Breakes through his baſer garments.

Hip. Hee's well got ſure.

Theſ. What made you ſeeke this place Sir?

Arc. Noble *Theſeus*.
To purchaſe name, and doe my ableſt ſervice
To ſuch a well-found wonder, as thy worth,
Fo onely in thy Court, of all the world
dwells faire-eyd honor.

Per. All his words are worthy.

Theſ. Sir, we are much endebted to your travell,
Nor ſhall you looſe your wiſh: *Perithous*
Diſpoſe of this faire Gentleman.

Perith. Thankes *Theſeus*.
What ere you are y'ar mine, and I ſhall give you
To a moſt noble ſervice, to this Lady,
This bright yong Virgin; pray obſerve her goodneſſe;
You have honourd hir faire birth-day, with your vertues,
And as your due y'ar hirs: kiſſe her faire hand Sir.

Arc. Sir, y'ar a noble Giver: deareſt Bewtie,
Thus let me ſeale my vowd faith: when your Servant
(Your moſt unworthie Creature) but offends you,
Command him die, he ſhall.

Emil. That were too cruell.
If you deſerve well Sir; I ſhall ſoone ſee't: (you,
Y'ar mine, aud ſomewhat better than your rancke Ile uſe

Per. Ile ſee you furniſh'd, and becauſe you ſay
You are a horſeman, I muſt needs intreat you
This after noone to ride, but tis a rough one.

Arc. I like him better (Prince) I ſhall not then
Freeze in my Saddle.

Theſ. Sweet, you muſt be readie,
And you *Emilia*, and you (Friend) and all
To morrow by the Sun, to doe obſervance
To flowry May, in *Dians* wood: waite well Sir
Vpon your Miſtris: *Emely*, I hope
He ſhall not goe a foote.

F   *Emil.*

Emil. That were a shame Sir,
While I have horses: take your choice,and what
You want at any time,let me but know it ;
If you serve faithfully,I dare assure you
You'l finde a loving Mistris.

Arc. If I doe not,
Let me finde that my Father ever hated,
Disgrace,and blowes.

Thes. Go leade the way; you have won it :
It shall be so ; you shall receave all dues
Fit for the honour you have won ; Twer wrong else,
Sister,beshrew my heart,you have a Servant,
That if I were a woman,would be Master,
But yon are wise. *Florish.*

Emil. I hope too wise for that Sir. *Exeunt omnes.*

Scæna 6. *Enter Iaylors Daughter alone.*

Daughter. Let all the Dukes,and all the divells rore,
He is at liberty : I have venturd for him,
And out I have brought him to a little wood
A mile hence,I have sent him,where a Cedar
Higher than all the rest,spreads like a plane
Fast by a Brooke,and there he shall keepe close,
Till I provide him Fyles,and foode,for yet
His yron bracelets are not off. O Love
What a stout hearted child thou art ! My Father
Durst better have indur'd cold yron,than done it:
I love him,beyond love,and beyond reason,
Or wit,or safetie : I have made him know it
I care not,I am desperate,If the law
Finde me,and then condemne me for't; some wenches,
Some honest harted Maides,will sing my Dirge.
And tell to memory,my death was noble,
Dying almost a Martyr : That way he takes,
I purpose is my way too : Sure he cannot
Be so unmanly,as to leave me here,
If he doe,Maides will not so easily
Trust men againe : And yet he has not thank'd me
For what I have done : no not so much as kist me,

And

And that (me thinkes) is not ſo well ; nor ſcarcely
Could I perſwade him to become a Freeman,
He made ſuch ſcruples of the wrong he did
To me, and to my Father. Yet I hope
When he conſiders more, this love of mine
Will take more root within him : Let him doe
What he will with me, ſo he uſe me kindly,
For uſe me ſo he ſhall, or ile proclaime him
And to his face, no-man : Ile preſently
Provide him neceſſaries, and packe my cloathes up,
And where there is a path of ground Ile venture
So hee be with me ; By him, like a ſhadow
Ile ever dwell; within this houre the whoobub
Will be all ore the priſon : I am then
Kiſſing the man they looke for : farewell Father;
Get many more ſuch priſoners, and ſuch daughters,
And ſhortly you may keepe your ſelfe.   Now to him.

Actus Tertius.

Scæna I. *Enter Arcite alone.*

Arcite. The Duke has loſt Hypolita; each tooke
A ſeverall land. This is a ſolemne Right
They owe bloomd May, and the *Athenians* pay it
To'th heart of Ceremony : O Queene *Emilia*
Freſher then May, ſweeter
Then hir gold Buttons on the bowes, or all
Th'en ſmelld knackes o'th Meade, or garden, yea
(We challenge too) the bancke of any Nymph
That makes the ſtreame ſeeme flowers; thou o Iewell
O'th wood, o'th world, haſt likewiſe bleſt a pace
With thy ſole preſence, in thy rumination
That I poore man might eftſoones come betweene
And chop on ſome cold thought, thrice bleſſed chance
To drop on ſuch a Miſtris, expectation
moſt giltleſſe on't : tell me O Lady Fortune
(Next after *Emely* my Soveraigne) how far

Cornets in
ſundry places.
Noiſe and
hallowing as
people a May-
ing:

I may be prowd. She takes ſtrong note of me,
Hath made me neere her ; and this beuteous Morne
(The prim'ſt of all the yeare)preſents me with
A brace of horſes,two ſuch Steeds might well
Be by a paire of Kings backt,in a Field
That their crownes titles tride : Alas,alas
Poore Coſen *Palamon,*poore priſoner,thou
So little dream'ſt upon my fortune,that
Thou thinkſt thy ſelfe, the happier thing,to be
So neare *Emilia,*me thou deem'ſt at *Thebs,*
And therein wretched,although free ; But if
Thou knew'ſt my Miſtris breathd on me,and that
I ear'd her language , livde in her eye; O Coz
What paſſion would encloſe thee.

*Enter Palamon as out of a Buſh, with his Shackles: bends
his fiſt at Arcite.*

  Palamon. Traytor kinſeman,
Thou ſhouldſt perceive my paſſion, if theſe ſignes
Of priſonment were off me,and this hand
But owner of a Sword : By all-othes in one
I, and the iuſtice of my love would make thee
A confeſt Traytor,o thou moſt perſidious
That ever gently lookd the voydes of honour.
That eu'r bore gentle. Token ; ſalſeſt Coſen
That ever blood made kin,call'ſt thou hir thine?
Ile prove it in my Shackles,with theſe hands,
Void of appointment,that thou ly'ſt,and art
A very theeſe in love,a Chaffy Lord
Nor worth the name of villaine : had I a Sword
And theſe houſe clogges away.
  Arc. Deere Coſin *Palamon,*
  Pal. Coſoner *Arcite,*give me language,ſuch
As thou haſt ſhewd me feate.
  Arc. Not finding in
The circuit of my breaſt, any groſſe ſtuffe
To forme me like your blazon,holds me to
This gentleneſſe of anſwer,tis your paſſion
That thus miſtakes,the which to you being enemy,
Cannot to me be kind : honor,and honeſtie

I cherish, and depend on, how so ev'r
You skip them in me, and with them faire Coz
Ile maintaine my proceedings; pray be pleas'd
To shew in generous termes, your griefes, since that
Your question's with your equall, who professes
To cleare his owne way, with the minde and Sword
Of a true Gentleman.

  Pal. That thou durst *Arcite.*

  Arc. My Coz, my Coz, you have beene well advertis'd
How much I dare, y'ave seene me use my Sword
Against th'advice of feare: sure of another
You would not heare me doubted, but your silence
Should breake out, though i'th Sanctuary.

  Pal. Sir,
I have seene you move in such a place, which well
Might justifie your manhood, you were calld   (faire
A good knight and a bold; But the whole weeke's not
If any day it rayne : Their valiant temper
Men loose when they encline to trecherie,
And then they fight like compelld Beares, would fly
Were they not tyde.

  Arc. Kinsman, you might as well
Speake this, and act it in your Glasse, as to
His eare, which now disdaines you.

  Pal. Come up to me,
Quit me of these cold Gyves, give me a Sword
Though it be rustie, and the charity
Of one meale lend me; Come before me then
A good Sword in thy hand, and doe but say
That *Emily* is thine, I will forgive
The trespasse thou hast done me, yea my life
If then thou carry't, and brave soules in shades
That have dyde manly, which will seeke of me
Some newes from earth, they shall get none but this
That thou art brave, and noble.

  Arc. Be content,
Againe betake you to your hawthorne house,
With counsaile of the night, I will be here
With wholesome viands; these impediments

                          Will

Will I file off, you shall have garments, and
Perfumes to kill the smell o'th prison, after
When you shall stretch your selfe, and say but *Arcite*
I am in plight, there shall be at your choyce
Both Sword, and Armour.

   Pal. Oh you heavens, dares any
So noble beare a guilty busines! none
But onely *Arcite*, therefore none but *Arcite*
In this kinde is so bold.

   Arc. Sweete *Palamon.*

   Pal. I doe embrace you, and your offer, for
Your offer doo't I onely, Sir your person
Without hipocrisy I may not wish

                Winde hornes of Cornets.

More then my Swords edge ont.

   Arc. You heare the Hornes;
Enter your Musicke least this match between's
Be crost, er met, give me your hand, farewell.
Ile bring you every needfull thing: I pray you
Take comfort and be strong.

   Pal. Pray hold your promise;
And doe the deede with a bent brow, most certaine
You love me not, be rough with me, and powre
This oile out of your language; by this ayre
I could for each word, give a Cuffe: my stomach
not reconcild by reason,

   Arc. Plainely spoken,
Yet pardon me hard language, when I spur

                    Winde hornes.

My horse, I chide him nor; content, and anger
In me have but one face. Harke Sir, they call
The scatterd to the Banket; you must guesse
I have an office there.

   Pal. Sir your attendance
Cannot please heaven, and I know your office
Vnjustly is atcheev'd.

   Arc. If a good title,
I am perswaded this question sicke between's,

By

By bleeding muſt be cur'd. I am a Suitour,
That to your Sword you will bequeath this plea,
And talke of it no more.

  Pal. But this one word:
You are going now to gaze upon my Miſtris,
For note you, mine ſhe is.

  Arc, Nay then.

  Pal. Nay pray you,
You talke of feeding me to breed me ſtrength
You are going now to looke upon a Sun
That ſtrengthens what it lookes on, there
You have a vantage ore me, but enjoy't till
I may enforce my remedy. Farewell.   *Exeunt.*

    Scæna 2. *Enter Iaylors daughter alone.*

  Daugh. He his miſtooke; the Beake I meant, is gone
After his fancy, Tis now welnigh morning,
No matter, would it were perpetuall night,
And darkenes Lord o'th world, Harke tis a woolfe:
In me hath greife ſlaine feare, and but for one thing
I care for nothing, and that's *Palamon.*
I wreake not if the wolves would jaw me, ſo
He had this File; what if I hallowd for him?
I cannot hallow: if I whoop'd; what then?
If he not anſweard, I ſhould call a wolfe,
And doe him but that ſervice. I have heard
Strange howles this live-long night, why may't not be
They have made prey of him? he has no weapons,
He cannot run, the Iengling of his Gives
Might call fell things to liſten, who have in them
A ſence to know a man unarmd, and can
Smell where reſiſtance is. Ile ſet it downe
He's torne to peeces, they howld many together
And then they feed on him: So much for that,
Be bold to ring the Bell; how ſtand I then?
All's char'd when he is gone, No, no I lye,
My Father's to be hang d for his eſcape,
My ſelfe to beg, if I prizd life ſo much
As to deny my act, but that I would not,

                        Should

Should I try death by duſſons; I am inop't,
Food tooke I none theſe two daies,
Sipt ſome water, I'have not cloſd mine eyes
Save when my lids ſcowrd off their bine; alas
Diſſolue my life, Let not my ſence unſettle
Leaſt I ſhould drowne, or ſtab, or hang my ſelfe,
O ſtate of Nature, faile together in me,
Since thy beſt props are warpt: So which way now?
The beſt way is, the next way to a grave:
Each errant ſtep beſide is torment. Loe
The Moone is down, the Cryckets chirpe, the Schreichowle
Calls in the dawne; all offices are done
Save what I faile in: But the point is this
An end, and that is all.   *Exit.*

Scæna 3. *Enter Arcite, with Meate, Wine and Files.*

Arc. I ſhould be neere the place, hoa. Coſen *Palamon.*
                                      Enter Palamon.

Pal. Arcite.

Arc. The ſame: I have brought you foode and files,
Come forth and feare not, her'es no *Theſeus.*

Pal. Nor none ſo honeſt *Arcite.*

Arc. That's no matter,
Wee'l argue that hereafter: Come-take courage,
You ſhall not dye thus beaſtly, here Sir drinke
I know you are faint, then le take further with you.

Pal. Arcite, thou mightſt now poyſon me.

Arc. I might.
But I muſt feare you firſt : Sit downe, and good now
No more of theſe vaine parlies; let us not
Having our anc ent reputation with us
Make talke for Fooles, and Cowards, To your health, &c.

Pal. Doe.

Arc. Pray ſit downe then, and let me entreate you
By all the honeſty and honour in you,
No mention of this woman, t'will diſturbe us,
We ſhall have time enough.

Pal. Well Sir, Ile pledge you.   (blood man.

Arc. Drinke a good hearty draught, it breeds good
                                                              Doe

Doe not you feele it thaw you?

Pal. Stay, Ile tell you after a draught or two more.

Arc. Spare it not, the Duke has more Cuz: Eate now.

Pal. Yes.

Arc. I am glad you have so good a stomach.

Pal. I am gladder I have so good meate too't,

Arc. Is't not mad lodging, here in the wild woods Cosen

Pal. Yes, for then that have wilde Consciences. (I see,

Arc. How tasts your vittails? your hunger needs no sawce

Pal. Not much.

But if it did, yours is too tart: sweete Cosen: what is this?

Arc. Venison.

Pal. Tis a lusty meate:

Giue me more wine; here *Arcite* to the wenches

We have known in our daies. The Lord Stewards daughter,

Doe you remember her?

Arc. After you Cuz.

Pal. She lov'd a black-haird man.

Arc. She did so; well Sir.

Pal. And I have heard some call him *Arcite*, and

Arc. Out with't faith.

Pal. She met him in an Arbour:

What did she there Cuz? play o'th virginals?

Arc. Something she did Sir.

Pal. Made her groane a moneth for't; or 2. or 3. or 10,

Arc. The Marshals Sister,

Had her share too, as I remember Cosen,

Else there be tales abroade, you'l pledge her?

Pal. Yes.

Arc. A pretty broune wench t'is-There was a time

When yong men went a hunting, and a wood,

And a broade Beech: and thereby hangs a tale: heigh ho.

Pal. For *Emily*, upon my life; Foole

Away with this straind mirth; I say againe

That sigh was breathd for *Emily*; base Cosen,

Dar'st thou breake first?

Arc. you are wide.

Pal. By heaven and earth, ther's nothing in thee honest,

G

Arc.

Arc, Then Ile leave you: you are a Beast now:

Pal. As thou makst me, Tray our.   (furnes:

Arc. Ther's all things needfull, files and shirts, and, per-
Ile come againe some two howres hence, and bring
That that shall quiet all,

Pal. A Sword and Armour:

Arc. Feare me not; you are now too fowle; farewell.
Get off your Trinkets, you shall want nought;

Pal. Sir ha:

Arc. Ile heare no more.   *Exit.*

Pal. If he keepe touch, he dies for't.   *Exit.*

Scæna 4. *Enter Iaylors daughter.*

Daugh. I am very cold, and all the Stars are out too,
The little Stars, and all, that looke like aglets:
The Sun has seene my Folly: *Palamon*;
Alas no; hees in heaven; where am I now?
Yonder's the sea, and ther's a Ship; how't tumbles
And ther's a Rocke lies watching under water;
Now, now, it beates upon it; now, now, new,
Ther's a leake sprung, a sound one, how they cry?
Vpon her before the winde, you'l loose all els:
Vp with a course or two, and take about Boyes.
Good night, good night, y'ar gons; I am very hungry,
Would I could finde a fine Frog; he would tell me
Newes from all parts o'th world, then would I make
A Carecke of a Cockle shell, and sayle
By east and North East to the King of *Pigmes*,
For he tels fortunes rarely. Now my Father
Twenty to one is trust up in a trice
To morrow morning, Ile say never a word.

Sing.   *For ile cut my greene coat, afoote above my knee,*
And ile clip my yellow lockes; an inch below mine eie.
                              hey, nonny, nonny, nonny,
He's buy me a white Cut, forth for to ride
And ile goe seeke him, throw the world that is so wide
                              hey nonny, nonny, nonny.

O for a pricke now like a Nightingale, to put my breast
                                        Against

Againſt. I ſhall ſleepe like a Top elſe.   *Exit.*
Scæna 6. *Enter a Schoole maſter.4. Countrymen:and*
Baum.2.or 3 wenches,with a Taborer.

Sch. Fy,fy,what tedioſity,& diſenſanity is here among ye?
have my Rudiments bin labourd ſo long with ye?milkd unto
ye, and by a figure even the very plumbroth & marrow of
my underſtanding laid upon ye? and do you ſtill cry where,
and how, & wherfore?you moſt courſe freeze capacities, ye
jaye Iudgements, have I ſaide thus let be, and there let be,
and then let be, and no man underſtand mee, *proh deum,*
medius ſidius, ye are all dunces: For why here ſtand I.
Here the Duke comes,there are you cloſe in the Thicket; the
Duke appeares, I meete him and unto him I utter learned
things,and many figures, he heares,and nods,and hums,and
then cries rare,and I goe forward,at length I fling my Gap
up;marke there; then do you as once did *Meleager,*an'd the
Bore break comly out before him:like true lovers,caſt your
ſelves in a Body decently,and ſweetly,by a figure trace,and
turne Boyes.
    1. And ſweetly we will doe it Maſter *Gerrold.*
    2. Draw up the Company,Where's the Taborour.
    3. Why *Timothy.*
Tab. Here my mad boyes,have at ye.
Sch. But I ſay where's their women?
    4. Here's *Friz* and *Maudline.*   *(Barbery.*
    2. And little *Luce* with the white legs, and bouncing
    1. And freckeled *Nel;* that never faild her Maſter.
*Sch.*Wher be your Ribands maids?ſwym with your Bodies
And carry it ſweetly, and deliverly
And now and then a fauour, and a friske.
Nel. Let us alone Sir.
Sch. Wher's the reſt o'th Muſicke.
    3. Diſperſd as you commanded.
Sch. Couple then
And ſee what's wanting;wher's the *Bavian?*
My friend,carry your taile without offence
Or ſcandall to the Ladies; and be ſure
You tumble with audacity,and manhood,

And when you barke doe it with judgement.

Bau. Yes Sir.

Sch. Quo usque tandem. Here is a woman wanting

4. We may goe whistle: all the fat's i'th fire.

Sch. We have,

As learned Authours utter, washd a Tile,

We have beene *fatuus,* and laboured vainely.

2. This is that scornefull peece, that scurvy hilding

That gave her promise faithfully, she would be here,

Cicely the Sempsters daughter:

The next gloves that I give her shall be dog skin;

Nay and she faile me once, you can tell *Arcas*

She swore by wine, and bread, she would not breake.

Sch. An Eele and woman,

A learned Poet sayes: unles by'th taile

And with thy teeth thou hold, will either faile,

In manners this was false position

2. A fire ill take her; do's she flinch now?

3.   What

Shall we determine Sir?

Sch. Nothing,

Our busines is become a nullity

Yea, and a woefull, and a pittious nullity.

4. Now when the credite of our Towne lay on it,

Now to be frampall, now to pisse o'th nettle,

Goe thy waies, ile remember thee, ile fit thee,

                                        Enter Iaylors daughter.

Daughter.

    The George alow, came from the South, from

    The coast of Barbary a.

    And there he met with brave gallants of war

             By one, by two, by three, a

    Well haild, well haild, you jolly gallants,

    And whither now are you bound a

Chaire and stooles out.

    O let me have your company till come to the sound a

    There was three fooles, fell out about an howlet

        The one sed it was an owle

       The other he sed nay,

The third he sed it was a hawke, and her bels wer cut away.

                      3. Ther's

3. Ther's a dainty mad woman Mr. comes i'th Nick as
mad as a march hare : if wee can get her daunce, wee are
made againe: I warrant her, shee'l doe the rarest gambols.

1. A mad woman? we are made Boyes.

Sch. And are you mad good woman?

Daugh. I would be sorry else,
Give me your hand.

Sch. Why?

Daugh. I can tell your fortune.
You are a foole : tell ten, I have pozd him : Buz
Friend you must eate no white bread, if you doe
Your teeth will bleede extreamely, shall we dance ho?
I know you, y'ar a Tinker: Sirha Tinker
Stop no more holes, but what you should.

Sch. Dij boni. A Tinker Damzell? (play

Daug. Or a Conjurer: raise me a devill now, and let him
Quipassa, o'th bels and bones.

Sch, Goe take her, aud fluently perswade her to a peace:
Et opus exegi, quod nec Iouis ira, nec ignis.
Strike up, and leade her in.

2. Come Lasse, lets trip it.

Daugh. Ile leade. (*Winde Hornes.*

3. Doe, doe.

Sch. Perswasively, and cunningly : away boyes,
Ex. all but Schoolemaster.

I heare the hornes : give me some
Meditation, and marke your Cue;
Pallas inspire me.

Enter Thes. Pir. Hip. Emil. Arcite: and traine.

Thes. This way the Stag tooke.

Sch. Stay, and edifie.

Thes. What have we here?

Per. Some Countrey sport, upon my life Sir.

Per. Well Sir, goe forward, we will edifie.
Ladies sit downe, wee'l stay it. (*Ladies.*

Sch. Thou doughtie Duke all haile: all haile sweet

Thes. This is a cold beginning.

Sch. If you but favour; our Country pastime made is,

We

We are a few of those collected here
That ruder Tongues distinguish villager,
And to say veritie, and not to fable;
We are a merry rout, or else a rable
Or company, or by a figure, *Choris*
That fore thy dignitie will dance a Morris.
And I that am the rectifier of all
By title Pedagogus, that let fall
The Birch upon the breeches of the small ones,
And humble with a Ferula the tall ones,
Doe here present this Machine, or this frame,
And daintie Duke, whose doughtie dismall fame
From *Dis* to *Dedalus*, from post to pillar
Is blowne abroad; helpe me thy poore well willer,
And with thy twinckling eyes, looke right and straight
Vpon this mighty Morr—of mickle waight
Is—now comes in, which being glewd together
Makes Morris, and the cause that we came hether.
The body of our sport of no small study
I first appeare, though rude, and raw, and muddy,
To speake before thy noble grace, this tenner:
At whose great feete I offer up my penner.
The next the Lord of May, and Lady bright,
The Chambermaid, and Servingman by night
That seeke out silent hanging: Then mine Host
And his fat Spowse, that welcomes to their cost
The gauled Traveller, and with a beckning
Informes the Tapster to inflame the reckning:
Then the beast eating Clowne, and next the foole,
The *Bavian* with long tayle, and eke long toole,
Cum multis aliys that make a dance,
Say I, and all shall presently advance.
  Thes. I, I by any meanes, deere Domine.
  Per. Produce.   *Musicke Dance.*

<table>
<tr><td>Knocke for
Schoole. Enter
The Dance.</td><td>*Intrate filij*, Come forth, and foot it,
Ladies, if we have beene merry
And have pleasd thee with a derry,
And a derry, and a downe</td></tr>
</table>

Say the Schoolemaster's no Clowne:
Duke, if we have pleasd thee too
And have done as good Boyes should doe,
Give us but a tree or twaine
For a Maypole, and againe
Ere another yeare run out,
Wee'l make thee laugh and all this rout.

 Thes. Take 20.Domine; how does my sweet heart.
 Hip. Never so pleasd Sir.
 Emil. Twas an excellent dance, and for a preface
I never heard a better.   (warded.
 Thes. Schoolemaster, I thanke yon, One see'em all re-
 Per. And heer's something to paint your Pole withall.
 Thes. Now to our sports againe.
 Sch. May the Stag thou huntst stand long,
And thy dogs be swift and strong :
May they kill him without lets,
And the Ladies eate his dowsets : Come we are all made.
         Winde Hornes.

Dij Deaq; omnes, ye have danc'd rarely wenches. *Exeunt.*
   Scæna 7. *Enter Palamon from the Bush.*
 Pal. About this houre my Cosen gave his faith
To visit me againe, and with him bring
Two Swords, and two good Armors; if he faile
He's neither man, nor Souldier ; when he left me
I did not thinke a weeke could have restord
My lost strength to me, I was growne so low,
And Crest-falne with my wants : I thanke thee *Arcite,*
Thou art yet a faire Foe ; and I feele my selfe
With this refreshing, able once againe
To out dure danger : To delay it longer
Would make the world think when it comes to hearing,
That I lay fatting like a Swine, to fight
And not a Souldier : Therefore this blest morning
Shall be the last ; and that Sword he refuses,
If it but hold, I kill him with; tis Iustice:
So love, and Fortune for me : O good morrow.
   Enter Arcite with Armors and Swords.
        Arcite.

Arc. Good morrow noble kinesman,

Pal. I have put you
To too much paines Sir.

Arc. That too much faire Cosen,
Is but a debt to honour, and my duty.

Pal. Would you were so in all Sir; I could wish ye
As kinde a kinsman, as you force me finde
A beneficiall foe, that my embraces
Might thanke ye, not my blowes.

Arc. I shall thinke either
Well done, a noble recompence.

Pal. Then I shall quit you.

Arc. Defy me in these faire termes, and you show
More then a Mistris to me, no more anger
As you love any thing that's honourable;
We were not bred to talke man, when we are arm'd
And both upon our guards, then let our fury
Like meeting of two tides, fly strongly from us,
And then to whom the birthright of this Beauty
Truely pertaines (without obbraidings, scornes,
Dispisings of our persons, and such powtings
Fitter for Girles and Schooleboyes) will be seene
And quickly, yours, or mine: wilt please you arme Sir,
Or if you feele your selfe not fitting yet
And furnishd with your old strength, ile stay Cosen
And ev'ry day discourse you into health,
As I am spard, your person I am friends with,
And I could wish I had not saide I lov'd her
Though I had dide; But loving such a Lady
And justifying my Love, I must not fly from't.

Pal. *Arcite*, thou art so brave an enemy
That no man but thy Cosen's fit to kill thee,
I am well, and lusty, choose your Armes.

Arc. Choose you Sir.

Pal. Wilt thou exceede in all, or do'st thou doe it
To make me spare thee?

Arc. If you thinke so Cosen,
You are deceived, for as I am a Soldier.

I

I will not spare you.

  Pal. That's well said.

  Arc. You'l finde it

  Pal. Then as I am an honest man and love,

With all the justice of affection

Ile pay thee soundly : This ile take.

  Arc. That's mine then,

Ile arme you first.

  Pal. Do : pray thee tell me Cosen,

Where got'st thou this good Armour.

  Arc : Tis the Dukes,

And to say true, I stole it; doe I pinch you?

  Pal. Noe.

  Arc. Is't not too heavie?

  Pal. I have worne a lighter,

But I shall make it serve.

  Arc. Ile buckl't close.

  Pal. By any meanes.

  Arc. You care not for a Grand guard?

  Pal. No, no, wee'l use no horses, I perceave

You would faine be at that Fight.

  Arc. I am indifferent.

  Pal. Faith so am I ; good Cosen, thrust the buckle

Through far enough.

  Arc. I warrant you.

  Pal. My Caske now.

  Arc. Will you fight bare-armd?

  Pal. We shall be the nimbler.

  Arc. But use your Gauntlets though; those are o'th least,

Prethee take mine good Cosen.

  Pal. Thanke you *Arcite.*

How doe I looke, am I falne much away?

  Arc. Faith very little ; love has usd you kindly.

  Pal. Ile warrant thee, Ile strike home.

  Arc. Doe, and spare not ;

Ile give you cause sweet Cosen.

  Pal. Now to you Sir,

Me thinkes this Armo'rs very like that, *Arcite,*

H

Thou

Thou wor'st that day the 3.Kings fell, but lighter.

Arc. That was a very good one, and that day
I well remember, you outdid me Cosen,
I never saw such valour: when you chargd
Vpon the left wing of the Enemie,
I spurd hard to come up, and under me
I had a right good horse.

Pal. You had indeede
A bright Bay I remember.

Arc. Yes but all
Was vainely labour'd in me, you outwent me,
Nor could my wishes reach you; yet a little
I did by imitation.

Pal. More by vertue,
You are modest Cosen.

Arc. When I saw you charge first,
Me thought I heard a dreadfull clap of Thunder
Breake from the Troope.

Pal. But still before that flew
The lightning of your valour; Stay a little,
Is not this peece too streight?

Arc. No, no, tis well.

Pal. I would have nothing hurt thee but my Sword,
A bruise would be dishonour.

Arc. Now I am perfect.

Pal. Stand off then.

Arc. Take my Sword, I hold it better.

Pal. I thanke ye: No, keepe it, your life lyes on it,
Here's one, if it but hold, I aske no more,
For all my hopes: My Cause and honour guard me.

They bow se-   *Arc.* And me my love: * Is there ought else to say?
verall wayes:
then advance   *Pal.* This onely, and no more: Thou art mine Aunts Son,
and stand.   And that blood we desire to shed is mutuall,
In me, thine, and in thee, mine: My Sword
Is in my hand, and if thou killst me
The gods, and I forgive thee; If there be
A place prepar'd for those that sleepe in honour,
I wish his wearie soule, that falls may win it:

                                                Fight

Fight bravely Cosen, give me thy noble hand.

Arc. Here *Palamon*: This hand shall never more
Come neare thee with such friendship.

Pal. I commend thee.

Arc. If I fall, curse me, and say I was a coward,
For none but such, dare die in these just Tryalls.
Once more farewell my Cosen,

Pal. Farewell *Arcite*.   *Fight.*

                     Hornes within:they stand.

Arc. Loe Cosen, loe, our Folly has undon us.

Pal. Why?

Arc. This is the Duke, a hunting as I told you,
If we be found, we are wretched, O retire
For honours sake, and safely presently
Into your Bush agen; Sir we shall finde
Too many howres to dye in, gentle Cosen:
If you be seene you perish instantly
For breaking prison, and I, if you reveale me,
For my contempt; Then all the world will scorne us,
And say we had a noble difference,
But base disposers of it.

  Pal. No, no, Cosen
I will no more be hidden, nor put off
This great adventure to a second Tryall
I know your cunning, and I know your cause,
He that faints now, shame take him, put thy selfe
Vpon thy present guard.

Arc. You are not mad?

Pal. Or I will make th'advantage of this howre
Mine owne, and what to come shall threaten me,
I feare lesse then my fortune: know weake Cosen
I love *Emilia*, and in that ile bury
Thee, and all crosses else.

Arc. Then come, what can come
Thou shalt know *Palamon*, I dare as well
Die, as discourse, or sleepe: Onely this feares me,
The law will have the honour of our ends.
Have at thy life.

Pal. Looke to thine owne well *Arcite.*

Fight againe.   *Hornes.*

Enter Thefeus, Hipolita, Emilia, Perithous and traine.

Thefeus. What ignorant and mad malicious Traitors,
Are you? That gainft the tenor of my Lawes
Are making Battaile, thus like Knights appointed,
Without my leave, and Officers of Armes?
By *Caftor* both fhall dye.

  Pal. Hold thy word *Thefeus,*
We are certainly both Traitors, both defpifers
Of thee, and of thy goodneffe: I am *Palamon*
That cannot love thee, he that broke thy Prifon,
Thinke well, what that deferves; and this is *Arcite*
A bolder Traytor never trod thy ground
A Falfer neu'r feem'd friend: This is the man
Was begd and banifh'd, this is he contemnes thee
And what thou dar'ft doe; and in this difguife
Againft this owne Edict followes thy Sifter,
That fortunate bright Star, the faire *Emilia*
Whofe fervant, (if there be a right in feeing,
And firft bequeathing of the foule to) juftly
I am, and which is more, dares thinke her his.
This treacherie like a moft trufty Lover,
I call'd him now to anfwer; if thou bee'ft
As thou art fpoken, great and vertuous,
The true defcider of all injuries,
Say, Fight againe, and thou fhalt fee me *Thefeus*
Doe fuch a Iuftice, thou thy felfe wilt envie,
Then take my life, Ile wooe thee too't.

  Per. O heaven,
What more then man is this!

  Thef. I have fworne.

  Arc. We feeke not
Thy breath of mercy *Thefeus,* Tis to me
A thing as foone to dye, as thee to fay it,
And no more mov'd: where this man calls me Traitor,
Let me fay thus much; if in love be Treafon,
In fervice of fo excellent a Beutie,

A3

As I love moft,and in that faith will perifh,
As I have brought my life here to confirme it,
As I have ferv'd her trueft,worthieft,
As I dare kill this Cofen, that denies it,
So let me be moft Traitor,and ye pleafe me :
For fcorning thy Edict Duke,aske that Lady
Why fhe is faire,and why her eyes command me
Stay here to love her; and if fhe fay Traytor,
I am a villaine fit to lye unburied.

    Pal. Thou fhalt have pitty of us both,o *Thefeus,*
If unto neither thou fhew mercy,ftop,
(As thou art juft) thy noble eare againft us,
As thou art valiant ; for thy Cofens foule
Whofe 12.ftrong labours crowne his memory,
Lets die together,at one inftant Duke,
Onely a little let him fall before me,
That I may tell my Soule he fhall not have her.

    Thef. I grant your wifh,for to fay true,your Cofen
Has ten times more offended,for I gave him
More mercy then you found,Sir,your offenfes
Being no more then his : None here fpeake for'em
For ere the Sun fet,both fhall fleepe for ever.

    Hipol. Alas the pitty,now or never Sifter
Speake not to be denide; That face of yours
Will beare the curfes elfe of after ages
For thefe loft Cofens.

    Emil. In my face deare Sifter
I finde no anger to'em;nor no ruyn,
The mifadventure of their owne eyes kill'em ;
Yet that I will be woman,and have pitty,
My knees fhall grow to'th ground but Ile get mercie,
Helpe me deare Sifter,in a deede fo vertuous,
The powers of all women will be with us,
Moft royall Brother.

    Hipol. Sir by our tye of Marriage.

    Emil, By your owne fpotleffe honour.

    Hip. By that faith,
That faire hand,and that honeft heart you gave me,

Emil.

Emil. By that you would have pitty in another,
By your owne vertues infinite.

Hip. By valour,
By all the chaste nights I have ever pleas'd you.

Thef. These are strange Conjurings.   (our dangers,

Per. Nay then I'oin too : By all our friendship Sir, by all
By all you love most, warres; and this sweet Lady.

Emil. By that you would have trembled to deny
A blushing Maide.

Hip. By your owne eyes : By strength
In which you swore I went beyond all women,
Almost all men, and yet I yeelded *Thefeus.*

Per. To crowne all this; By your most noble soule
Which cannot want due mercie, I beg first.

Hip. Next heare my prayers.

Emil. Last let me intreate Sir.

Per. For mercy.

Hip. Mercy.

Emil. Mercy on these Princes.

Thef. Ye make my faith reele : Say I felt
Compassion to'em both, how would you place it ?

Emil. Vpon their lives : But with their banishments.

Thef. You are a right woman, Sister you have pitty,
But want the vnderstanding where to use it.
If you desire their lives, invent a way
Safer then banishment : Can these two live
And have the agony of love about 'em,
And not kill one another? Every day
The'yld fight about yov ; howrely bring your honour
In publique question with their Swords ; Be wise then
And here forget 'em; it concernes your credit,
And my oth equally : I have said they die,
Better they fall by'th law, then one another.
Bow not my honor.

Emil. O my noble Brother,
That oth was rashly made, and in your anger,
Your reason will not hold it, if such vowes
Stand for expresse will, all the world must perish.

Beside

Beside, I have another oth, gainst yours
Of more authority, I am sure more love,
Not made in passion neither, but good heede.

 Thes. What is it Sister?

 Per. Vrge it home brave Lady.

 Emil. That you would nev'r deny me any thing
Fit for my modest suit, and your free granting:
I tye you to your word now, if ye fall in't,
Thinke how you maime your honour;
(For now I am set a begging Sir, I am deafe
To all but your compassion) how their lives
Might breed the ruine of my name; Opinion,
Shall any thing that loves me perish for me?
That were a cruell wisedome, doe men proyne
The straight yong Bowes that blush with thousand Blossoms
Because they may be rotten? O Duke *Thesens*
The goodly Mothers that have groand for these,
And all the longing Maides that ever lov'd,
If your vow stand, shall curse me and my Beauty,
And in their funerall songs, for these two Cosens
Despise my crueltie, and cry woe worth me,
Till I am nothing but the scorne of women;
For heavens sake save their lives, and banish 'em.

 Thes. On what conditions?

 Emil. Sweare 'em never more
To make me their Contention, or to know me,
To tread upon thy Dukedome, and to be
Where ever they shall travel, ever strangers to one another.

 Pal. Ile be cut a peeces
Before I take this oth, forget I love her?
O all ye gods dispise me then: Thy Banishment
I not mislike, so we may faire'y carry
Our Swords, and cause along: else never trifle,
But take our lives Duke, I must love and will,
And for that love, must and dare kill this Cosen
On any peece the earth has.

 Thes. Will you *Arcite*
Take these conditions?

           Pal.

Pal. H'es a villaine then.

Per. Thefe are men.

Arcite. No, never Duke: Tis worfe to me than begging
To take my life fo bafely, though I thinke
I never fhall enjoy her, yet ile preferve
The honour of affection, and dye for her,
Make death a Devill.

   Thef. What may be done? for now I feele compaffion.

Per. Let it not fall agen Sir.

   Thef. Say *Emilia*
If one of them were dead, as one muft, are you
Content to take th'other to your husband?
They cannot both enjoy you; They are Princes
As goodly as your owne eyes, and as noble
As ever fame yet fpoke of; looke upon'em,
And if you can love, end this difference,
I give confent, are you content too Princes?

   Both. With all our foules.

   Thef. He that fhe refufes
Muft dye then.

   Both. Any death thou canft invent Duke.

   Pal. If I fall from that mouth, I fall with favour,
And Lovers yet unborne fhall bleffe my afhes.

   Arc. If fhe refufe me, yet my grave will wed me,
And Souldiers fing my Epitaph.

   Thef. Make choice then.

   Emil. I cannot Sir, they are both too excellent
For me, a hayre fhall never fall of thefe men.

   Hip. What will become of 'em?

   Thef. Thus I ordaine it,
And by mine honor, once againe it ftands,
Or both fhall dye. You fhall both to your Conntrey,
And each within this moneth accompanied
With three faire Knights, appeare againe in this place,
In which Ile plant a Pyramid; and whether
Before us that are here, can force his Cofen
By fayre and knightly ftrength to touch the Pillar,
He fhall enjoy her: the other loofe his head,

And all his friends; Nor shall he grudge to fall,
Nor thinke he dies with interest in this Lady:
Will this content yee?
  Pal. Yes:here Cosen *Arcite*
I am friends againe, till that howre.
  Arc. I embrace ye.
  Thes. Are you content Sister?
  Emil. Yes, I must Sir,
Els both miscarry.
  Thes. Come shake hands againe then,
And take heede, as you are Gentlemen,this Quarrell
Sleepe till the howre prefixt, and hold your course.
  Pal. We dare not faile thee *Theseus.*
  Thes. Come, Ile give ye
Now usage like to Princes,and to Friends:
When ye returne, who wins,Ile settle heere,
Who looses,yet Ile weepe upon his Beere.   *Exeunt.*

Actus Quartus.

Scæna I. *Enter Iailor, and his friend.*
Iailor. Heare you no more,was nothing saide of me
Concerning the escape of *Palamon*?
Good Sir remember.
  1.*Fr.* Nothing that I heard,
For I came home before the busines
Was fully ended: Yet I might perceive
Ere I departed, a great likelihood
Of both their pardons:For *Hipolita,*
And faire-eyd *Emilie,*upon their knees
Begd with such hansom pitty,that the Duke
Methought stood staggering,whether he should follow
His rash o'th,or the sweet compassion
Of those two Ladies;and to second them,
That truely noble Prince *Perithous*
Halfe his owne heart, set in too,that I hope
All shall be well: Neither heard I one question
                    I   Of

Of your name, or his scape.   *Enter 2. Friend.*

Iay. Pray heaven it hold so.

2. *Fr:* Be of good comfort man ; I bring you newes,
Good newes.

Iay. They are welcome,

2. *Fr.* *Palamon* has cleerd you,
And got your pardon, and discoverd   (Daughters,
How, and by whose meanes he escapt, which was your
Whose pardon is procurd too, and the Prisoner
Not to be held ungratefull to her goodnes,
Has given a summe of money to her Marriage,
A large one ile assure you.

Iay. Ye are a good man
And ever bring good newes.

1. *Fr.* How was it ended?

2. *Fr.* Why, as it should be; they that nev'r begd
But they prevaild, had their suites fairely granted,
The prisoners have their lives.

1. *Fr.* I knew t'would be so.

2. *Fr.* But there be new conditions, which you'l heare of
At better time.

Iay. I hope they are good.

2. *Fr.* They are honourable,
How good they'l prove, I know not.

                                        Enter Wooer.

1. *Fr.* T'will be knowne.

Woo. Alas Sir, wher's your Daughter?

Iay. Why doe you aske?

Woo. O Sir when did you see her?

2. *Fr.* How he lookes?

Iay. This morning.   (she sleepe?

Woo. Was she well? was she in health? Sir, when did

1. *Fr.* These are strange Questions.

Iay. I doe not thinke she was very well, for now
You make me minde her, but this very day
I ask'd her questions, and she answered me
So farre from what she was, so childishly,
So sillily, as if she were a foole,

                                                    An

An Inocent,and I was very angry.
But what of her Sir ?   (as good by me

Woo. Nothing but my pitty;but you muſt know it,and
As by an other that leſſe loves her:

Iay. Well Sir.

1.Fr. Not right ?

2.Fr. Not well ? ――――*Wooer*, No Sir not well.

*Woo.*Tis too true, ſhe is mad.

1.Fr. It cannot be.

Woo. Beleeve you'l finde it ſo.

*Iay.*I halfe ſuſpeĉted
What you told me: the gods comfort her :
Either this was her love to *Palamon*,
Or feare of my miſcarrying on his ſcape,
Or both.

    Woo. Tis likely.

    Iay. But why all this haſte Sir ?

    Woo. Ile tell you quickly. As I late was angling
In the great Lake that lies behind the Pallace ,
From the far ſhore, thicke ſet with reedes, and Sedges,
As patiently I was attending ſport,
I heard a voyce,a ſhrill one,and attentive
I gave my eare, when I might well perceive
T'was one that ſung,and by the ſmallneſſe of it
A boy or woman. I then left my angle
To his owne skill, came neere, but yet perceivd not
Who made the ſound ; the ruſhes,and the Reeds
Had ſo encompaſt it : I laide me downe
And liſtned to the words ſhe ſong, for then
Through a ſmall glade cut by the Fiſher men,
I ſaw it was your Daughter.

    Iay. Pray goe on Sir ?

    Woo. She ſung much, but no ſence; onely I heard her
Repeat this often.*Palamon* is gone,
Is gone to'th wood to gather Mulberies,
Ile finde him out to morrow.

    1.Fr. Pretty ſoule.

    Woo. His ſhackles will betray him, hee'l be taken,

And what shall I doe then? Ile bring a beavy,
A hundred blacke eyd Maides, that love as I doe
With Chaplets on their heads of Daffadillies,
With cherry-lips, and cheekes of Damaske Roses,
And all wee'l daunce an Antique fore the Duke,
And beg his pardon; Then she talk'd of you Sir;
That you must loose your head to morrow morning,
And she must gather flowers to bury you,
And see the house made handsome, then she sung
Nothing but Willow, willow, willow, and betweene
Ever was, *Palamon*, faire *Palamon*,
And *Palamon*, was a tall yong man. The place
Was knee deepe where she sat; her careles Tresses,
A wreake of bull-rush rounded; about her stucke
Thousand fresh water flowers of severall cullors.
That me thought she appeard like the faire Nimph
That feedes the lake with waters, or as Iris
Newly dropt downe from heaven; Rings she made
Of rushes that grew by, and to 'em spoke
The prettiest posies: Thus our true love's tide,
This you may loose, not me, and many a one:
And then she wept, and sung againe, and sigh'd,
And with the same breath smil'd, and kist her hand,
    2. *Fr.* Alas what pitty it is?
    Wooer. I made in to her.
She saw me, and straight sought the flood, I sav'd her,
And set her safe to land: when presently
She slipt away, and to the Citty made,
With such a cry, and swiftnes, that beleeve me
Shee left me farre behinde her; three, or foure,
I saw from farre off crosse her, one of 'em
I knew to be your brother, where she staid,
And fell, scarce to be got away: I left them with her.
                    Enter Brother, Daughter, and others.
And hether came to tell you: Here they are.
    Daugh. May you never more enjoy the light, &c.
Is not this a fine Song?
    Bro. O a very fine one.

                                        Daugh.

Daugh. I can sing twenty more.

Bro. I thinke you can,

Daugh. Yes truely can I, I can sing the Broome,
And Bony Robin. Are not you a tailour?

Bro. Yes,

Daugh. Wher's my wedding Gowne?

Bro. Ile bring it to morrow.

Daugh. Doe, very rarely, I must be abroad else
To call the Maides, and pay the Minstrels
For I must loose my Maydenhead by cocklight
Twill never thrive else.

    O faire, oh sweete, &c.   *Singes.*

Bro. You must ev'n take it patiently.

Iay. Tis true,

Daugh. Good'ev'n, good men, pray did you ever heare
Of one yong *Palamon?*

Iay. Yes wench we know him.

Daugh. Is't not a fine yong Gentleman?

Iay. Tis, Love.

Bro. By no meane crosse her, she is then distemperd
Far worse then now she showes.

  1. Fr. Yes, he's a fine man.

Daugh. O, is he so? you have a Sister.

  1. Fr. Yes.

Daugh. But she shall never have him, tell her so,
For a tricke that I know, y'had best looke to her,
For if she see him once, she's gone, she's done,
And undon in an howre. All the young Maydes
Of our Towne are in love with him, but I laugh at 'em
And let 'em all alone, Is't not a wise course?

  1. Fr. Yes.   (by him,

Daugh. There is at least two hundred now with child
There must be fowre; yet I keepe close for all this,
Close as a Cockle; and all these must be Boyes,
He has the tricke on't, and at ten yeares old
They must be all gelt for Musitians,
And sing the wars of *Theseu.*

  2. Fr. This is strange.

          I 3   *Daugh.*

Daugh. As ever you heard, but say nothing.

1. *Fr.* No.   (him,

Daugh. They come from all parts of the Dukedome to

Ile warrant ye, he had not so few last night

As twenty to dispatch, hee'l tickl't up

In two howres, if his hand be in.

  Iay. She's lost

Past all cure.

  Bro. Heaven forbid man.

  Daugh. Come hither, you are a wise man.

  1. *Fr.* Do's she know him?

  1. *Fr.* No, would she did.

  Daugh. You are master of a Ship?

  Iay. Yes.

  Daugh. Wher's your Compasse?

  Iay. Heere.

  Daugh. Set it too'th North.

And now direct your course to'th wood, wher *Palamon*

Lyes longing for me; For the Tackling

Let me alone; Come waygh my hearts, cheerely.

  All. Owgh, owgh, owgh, tis up, the wind's faire, top the

Bowling, out with the maine saile, wher's your

Whistle Master?

  Bro. Lets get her in.

  Iay. Vp to the top Boy.

  Bro. Wher's the Pilot?

  1. *Fr.* Heere,

  Daugh. What ken'st thou?

  2. *Fr.* A faire wood.

  Daugh. Beare for it master: take about :   *Singes.*

When Cinthia with her borrowed light, &c.   *Exeunt.*

    Scæna 2. *Enter Emilia alone, with 2, Pictures.*

  Emilia. Yet I may binde those wounds up, that must

And bleed to death for my sake else; Ile choose,   (open

And end their strife: Two such yong hausom men

Shall never fall for me, their weeping Mothers,

Following the dead cold ashes of their Sonnes

Shall never curse my cruelty: Good heaven,

                                           What

What a sweet face has *Arcite* ? if wise nature
With all her best endowments, all those beuties
She sowes into the birthes of noble bodies,
Were here a mortall woman, and had in her
The coy denialls of yong Maydes, yet doubtles,
She would run mad for this man: what an eye ?
Of what a fyry sparkle, and quick sweetnes,
Has this yong Prince? Here Love himselfe sits smyling,
Iust such another wanton *Ganimead*,
Set Love a fire with, and enforcd the god
Snatch up the goodly Boy, and set him by him
A shining constellation: What a brow,
Of what a spacious Majesty he carries ?
Arch'd like the great eyd *Iuno's*, but far sweeter,
Smoother then *Pelops* Shoulder ? Fame and honour
Me thinks from hence, as from a Promontory
Pointed in heaven, should clap their wings, and sing
To all the under world, the Loves, and Fights
Of gods, and such men neere 'em. *Palamon*,
Is but his foyle, to him, a meere dull shadow,
Hee's swarth, and meagre, of an eye as heavy
As if he had lost his mother ; a still temper,
No stirring in him, no alacrity,
Of all this sprightly sharpenes, not a smile ;
Yet these that we count errours may become him :
Narcissu was a sad Boy, but a heavenly :
Oh who can finde the bent of womans fancy ?
I am a Foole, my reason is lost in me,
I have no choice, and I have ly'd so lewdly
That women ought to beate me. On my knees
I aske thy pardon : *Palamon*, thou art alone,
And only beutifull, and these the eyes,
These the bright lamps of beauty, that command
And threaten Love, and what yong Mayd dare crosse 'em
What a bold gravity, and yet inviting
Has this browne manly face ? O Love, this only
From this howre is Complexion: Lye there *Arcite*,
Thou art a changling to him, a meere Gipsey,

Aad

And this the noble Bodie: I am sotted,
Vtterly lost: My Virgins faith has fled me.
For if my brother but even now had ask'd me
Whether I lov'd, I had run mad for *Arcite*,
Now if my Sister; More for *Palamon*,
Stand both together: Now, come aske me Brother,
Alas, I know not: aske me now sweet Sister,
I may goe looke; What a meere child is *Fancie*,
That having two faire gawdes of equall sweetnesse,
Cannot distinguish, but must crie for both.

　　　　　　　　　　　　　Enter Emil. and Gent:

　Emil. How now Sir?
　Gent. From the Noble Duke your Brother
Madam, I bring you newes: The Knights are come.
　Emil. To end the quarrell?
　Gent. Yes.
　Emil. Would I might end first:
What sinnes have I committed, chast *Diana*,
That my unspotted youth must now be soyld
With blood of *Princes*? and my Chastitie
Be made the Altar, where the lives of Lovers,
Two greater, and two better never yet
Made mothers joy, must be the sacrifice
To my unhappy Beautie?

　　　　Enter Theseus, Hipolita, Perithous and attendants.
　Theseus. Bring 'em in quickly,
By any meanes, I long to see 'em.
Your two contending Lovers are return'd,
And with them their faire Knights: Now my faire Sister,
You must love one of them.
　Emil. I had rather both,
So neither for my sake should fall untimely

　　　　　　　　　　　Enter Messengers. Curtis.

　Thes. Who saw 'em?
　Per. I a while.
　Gent. And I.
　Thes. From whence come you Sir?
　Mess. From the Knights.

　　　　　　　　　　　　　　　　　Thes.

Thef. Pray fpeake
You that have feene them, what they are.

Mef. I will Sir,
And truly what I thinke : Six braver fpirits
Then thefe they have brought, (if we judge by the outfide)
I never faw, nor read of : He that ftands
In the firft place with *Arcite*, by his feeming
Should be a ftout man, by his face a Prince,
(His very lookes fo fay him) his complexion,
Nearer a browne, than blacke; fterne, and yet noble,
Which fhewes him hardy, fearcleffe, proud of dangers:
The circles of his eyes fhow faire within him,
And as a heated Lyon, fo he lookes ;
His haire hangs long behind him, blacke and fhining
Like Ravens wings : his fhoulders broad, and ftrong,
Armd long and round, and on his Thigh a Sword
Hung by a curious Bauldricke ; when he frownes
To feale his will with, better o'my confcience
Was never Souldiers friend.

Thef. Thou ha'ft well defcribde him,

Per. Yet a great deale fhort
Me thinkes, of him that's firft with *Palamon.*

Thef. Pray fpeake him friend.

Per. I gheffe he is a Prince too,
And if it may be, greater; for his fhow
Has all the ornament of honour in't:
Hee's fomewhat bigger, then the Knight he fpoke of,
But of a face far fweeter ; His complexion
Is (as a ripe grape) ruddy : he has felt
Without doubt what he fights for, and fo apter
To make this caufe his owne : In's face appeares
All the faire hopes of what he undertakes,
And when he's angry, then a fetled valour
(Not tainted with extreames) runs through his body,
And guides his arme to brave things : Feare he cannot,
He fhewes no fuch foft temper, his head's yellow,
Hard hayr'd, and curld, thicke twind like Ivy tops,
Not to undoe with thunder ; In his face

K   The

The liverie of the warlike Maide appeares,
Pure red, and white, for yet no beard has bleſt him.
And in his rowling eyes, ſits victory,
As if ſhe ever ment to corect his valour:
His Noſe ſtands high, a Character of honour.
His red lips, after fights, are fit for Ladies.

    Emil. Muſt theſe men die too?

    Per. When he ſpeakes, his tongue
Sounds like a Trumpet; All his lyneaments
Are as a man would wiſh 'em, ſtrong, and cleane,
He weares a well-ſteeld Axe, the ſtaffe of gold,
His age ſome five and twenty.

    Meſſ. Ther's another,
A little man, but of a tough ſoule, ſeeming
As great as any: fairer promiſes
In ſuch a Body, yet I never look'd on.

    Per. O, he that's freckle fac'd?

    Meſſ The ſame my Lord,
Are they not ſweet ones?

    Per. Yes they are well.

    Meſſ. Me thinkes,
Being ſo few, and well diſpoſd, they ſhow
Great, and fine art in nature, he's white hair'd,
Not wanton white, but ſuch a manly colour
Next to an aborne, tough, and nimble ſet,
Which ſhowes an active ſoule; his armes are brawny
Linde with ſtrong ſinewes: To the ſhoulder peece,
Gently they ſwell, like women new conceav'd,
Which ſpeakes him prone to labour, never fainting
Vnder the waight of Armes; ſtout harted, ſtill,
But when he ſtirs, a Tiger; he's gray eyd,
Which yeelds compaſſion where he conquers: ſharpe
To ſpy advantages, and where he finds 'em,
He's ſwift to make 'em his: He do's no wrongs,
Nor takes none; he's round fac'd, and when he ſmiles
He ſhowes a Lover, when he frownes, a Souldier:
About his head he weares the winners oke,
And in it ſtucke the ſavour of his Lady:

His

His age, some six and thirtie. In his hand
He beares a charging Staffe, embost with silver.

Thef. Are they all thus?

Per. They are all the sonnes of honour.

Thef. Now as I have a soule I long to see'em,
Lady you shall see men fight now.

Hip. I wish it,
But not the cause my Lord ; They would show
Bravely about the Titles of two Kingdomes ;
Tis pitty Love should be so tyrannous :
O my soft harted Sister, what thinke you ?
Weepe not, till they weepe blood ; Wench it must be.

Thef. You have steel'd 'em with your Beautie : honord
To you I give the Feild ; pray order it,   (Friend,
Fitting the persons that must use it.

Per. Yes Sir.

Thef. Come, Ile goe visit 'em : I cannot stay.
Their fame has fir'd me so ; Till they appeare,
Good Friend be royall.

Per. There shall want no bravery.

Emilia. Poore wench goe weepe, for whosoever wins,
Looses a noble Cosen, for thy sins.   *Exeunt.*

Scæna 3. *Enter Iailor, Wooer, Doctor.*

Doct. Her distraction is more at some time of the Moone,
Then at other some, is it not ?

Iay. She is continually in a harmelesse distemper, sleepes
Little, altogether without appetite, save often drinking,
Dreaming of another world, and a better; and what
Broken peece of matter so'ere she's about, the name
Palamon lardes it, that she farces ev'ry busines

Enter Daughter.

Withall, fyts it to every question ; Looke where
Shee comes, you shall perceive her behaviour.

Daugh. I have forgot it quite; The burden o'nt, was *downe*
A downe a; and pend by no worse man, then
Giraldo, Emilias Schoolemaster; he's as
Fantasticall too, as ever he may goe upon's legs,
For in the next world will *Dido* see *Palamon*, and

K 2   Then

Then will she be out of love with *Eneas.*

Doct. What stuff's here? pore soule.

Ioy. Ev'n thus all day long.

Daugh. Now for this Charme, that I told you of, you must
Bring a peece of silver on the tip of your tongue,
Or no ferry; then if it be your chance to come where
The blessed spirits, as the'rs a sight now; we maids
That have our Lyvers, perish'd, crakt to peeces with
Love, we shall come there, and doe nothing all day long
But picke flowers with Proserpine, then will I make
Palamon a Nosegay, then let him marke me,——then.

Doct. How prettily she's amisse? note her a little further.

Dau. Faith ile tell you, sometime we goe to Barly breake,
We of the blessed; alas, tis a sore life they have i'th
Thother place, such burning, frying, boyling, hissing,
Howling, chattring, cursing, oh they have shrowd
Measure, take heede; if one be mad, or hang or
Drowne themselves, thither they goe, *Iupiter* blesse
Vs, and there shall we be put in a Caldron of
Lead, and Vsurers grease, amongst a whole million of
Cutpurses, and there boyle like a Gamon of Bacon
That will never be enough.   *Exit.*

Doct. How her braine coynes?

Daugh. Lords and Courtiers, that have got maids with
Child, they are in this place, they shall stand in fire up to the
Nav'le, and in yce up to'th hart, and there th'offending part
burnes, and the deceaving part freezes; in troth a very gree-
vous punishment, as one would thinke, for such a Trifle, be-
leve me one would marry a leaprous witch, to be rid on't
Ile assure you.

Doct. How she continues this fancie? Tis not an engraffed
Madnesse, but a most thicke, and profound mellencholly.

Daugh. To heare there a proud Lady, and a proud Citty
wiffe, howle together: I were a beast and il'd call it good
sport: one cries, o this smoake, another this fire; One cries, o,
that ever I did it behind the arras, and then howles; th'other
curses a suing fellow and her garden house.

Sings. *I will be true, my stars, my fate, &c.*   *Exit Daugh.*
                                                         Iaylor.

Iay. What thinke you of her Sir? (minister to.

Doct. I think she has a perturbed minde, which I cannot

   Iay. Alas, what then?

Doct. Vnderstand you, she ever affected any man, ere
She beheld *Palamon*?

   Iay. I was once Sir, in great hope, she had fixd her
Liking on this gentleman my friend. (great

   Woo. I did thinke so too, and would account I had a
Pen-worth on't, to give halfe my state, that both
She and I at this present stood unfainedly on the
Same tearmes. (the

   Do. That intemprat surfeit of her eye, hath distemperd
Other sences, they may returne and settle againe to
Execute their preordaind faculties, but they are
Now in a most extravagant vagary. This you
Must doe, Confine her to a place, where the light
May rather seeme to steale in, then be permitted; take
Vpon you (yong Sir her friend) the name of
Palamon, say you come to eate with her, and to
Commune of Love; this will catch her attention, for
This her minde beates upon; other objects that are
Inserted tweene her minde and eye, become the prankes
And friskins of her madnes; Sing to her, such greene
Songs of Love, as she sayes *Palamon* hath sung in
Prison; Come to her, stucke in as sweet flowers, as the
Season is mistres of, and thereto make an addition of
Som other compounded odours, which are gratefull to the
Sence: all this shall become *Palamon*, for *Palamon* can
Sing, and *Palamon* is sweet, and ev'ry good thing, desire
To eate with her, crave her, drinke to her, and still
Among, intermingle your petition of grace and acceptance
Into her favour: Learne what Maides have beene her
Companions, and play-pheeres, and let them repaire to
Her with *Palamon* in their mouthes, and appeare with
Tokens, as if they suggested for him, It is a falsehood
She is in, which is with falsehoods to be combated.
This may bring her to eate, to sleepe, and reduce what's
Now out of square in her, into their former law, and

Regiment,

Regiment; I have seene it approved, how many times
I know not, but to make the number more, I have
Great hope in this. I will betweene the passages of
This project, come in with my applyance: Let us
Put it in execution; and hasten the successe, which doubt not
Will bring forth comfort.   *Florish. Exeunt.*

Actus Quintus.

Scæna 1. *Enter Thesius, Perithous, Hipolita, attendants.*
   Thes. Now let'em enter, and before the gods
Tender their holy prayers: Let the Temples
Burne bright with sacred fires, and the Altars
In hallowed clouds commend their swelling Incense
To those above us: Let no due be wanting,
                              Florish of Cornets.
They have a noble worke in hand, will honour
The very powers that love 'em.
                   Enter Palamon and Arcite, and their Knights.
   Per. Sir they enter.
   Thes. You valiant and strong harted Enemies
You royall German foes, that this day come
To blow that nearenesse out that flames betweene ye;
Lay by your anger for an houre, and dove-like
Before the holy Altars of your helpers
(The all feard gods) bow downe your stubborne bodies,
Your ire is more than mortall; So your helpe be,
And as the gods regard ye, fight with Iustice,
I le leave you to your prayers, and betwixt ye
I part my wishes.
   Per. Honour crowne the worthiest.
                              Exit Thesens, and his traine.
   Pal. The glasse is running now that cannot finish
Till one of us expire: Thinke you but thus,
That were there ought in me which strove to show
Mine enemy in this businesse, wer't one eye
Against another: Arme opprest by Arme:

I

I would destroy th'offender, Coz, I would
Though parcell of my selfe : Then from this gather
How I should tender you.

 Are. I am in labour
To push your name, your auncient love, our kindred
Out of my memory; and i'th selfe same place
To seate something I would confound : So hoyst we
The sayles, that must these vessells port even where
The heavenly Lymiter pleases.

 Pal. You speake well;
Before I turne, Let me embrace thee Cosen
This I shall never doe agen.

  Arc. One farewell.

 Pal. Why let it be so : Farewell Coz.
      Exeunt Palamon and his Knights.

 Arc. Farewell Sir;
Knights, Kinsemen, Lovers, yea my Sacrifices
True worshippers of Mars, whose spirit in you
Expells the seedes of feare, and th'apprehension
Which still is farther off it; Goe with me
Before the god of our profession : There
Require of him the hearts of Lyons, and
The breath of Tigers, yea the fearcenesse too,
Yea the speed also, to goe on, I meane:
Else wish we to be Snayles ; you know my prize
Must be drag'd out of blood, force and great feate
Must put my Garland on, where she stickes
The Queene of Flowers: our intercession then
Must be to him that makes the Campe, a Cestron
Brymd with the blood of men : give me your aide
And bend your spirits towards him.   *They kneele.*
Thou mighty one, that with thy power hast turnd
Greene Nepture into purple.
Comets prewarne, whose havocke in vaste Feild
Vnearthed skulls proclaime, whose breath blowes downe,
The teeming Ceres foyzon, who dost plucke
With hand armenypotent from forth blew clowdes,
The masond Turrets, that both mak'it, and break'st

          The

The ſtony girthes ofCittiesːme thy puple,
Yongeſt follower of thy Drom,inſtruct this day
With military skiil,that to thy lawde
I may advance my Streamer,and by thee,
Be ſtil'd the Lord o'th day,give me great Mars
Some token of thy pleaſure.

Here they fall on their faces as formerly,and there is heard
elanging of Armor,with a ſport Thunder as the burſt of
a Bastaile,whereupon they all riſe and bow to the Altar.

O Great Corrector of enormous times,
Shaker ofore-rank States, thou grand decider
Of duſtie,and old tytles,that healſt with blood
The earth when it is ſicke,and curſt the world
O'th plureſie of people; I doe take
Thy ſignes auſpiciouſly,and in thy name
To my deſigne ; march boldly,let us goe.   *Exeunt.*

Enter Palamon and his Knights, with the former obſer-
vance.

  Pal. Our ſtars muſt gliſter with new fire,or be
To daie extinct;our argument is love,
Which if the goddeſſe of it grant,ſhe gives
Victory too,then blend your ſpirits with mine,
You,whoſe free nobleneſſe doe make my cauſe
Your perſonall hazard ; to the goddeſſe *Venus*
Commend we our proceeding,and implore
Her power unto our partie.   *Here they kneele as formerly.*
Haile Soveraigne Queene of ſecrets,who haſt power
To call the ſeirceſt Tyrant from his rage ;
And weepe unto a Girle; that ha'ſt the might
Even with an ey-glance,to choke *Marſis* Drom
And turne th'allarme to whiſpers,that canſt make
A Criple floriſh with his Crutch,and cure him,
Before *Apollo*;that may'ſt force the King
To be his ſubjects vaſſaile,and induce
Stale gravitie to daunce,the pould Bachelour
Whoſe youth like wanton Boyes through Bonfyres
Have skipt thy flame,at ſeaventy,thou canſt catch
And make him to the ſcorne of his hoarſe throate

                                                      Abuſe

Abuse yong laies of love; what godlike power
Haft thou not power upon? To *Phebus* thou
Add'ft flames, hotter then his the heavenly fyres
Did fcortch his mortall Son, thine him; the huntreffe
All moyft and cold, fome fay began to throw
Her Bow away, and figh: take to thy grace
Me thy vowd Souldier, who doe beare thy yoke
As t'wer a wreath of Rofes, yet is heavier
Then Lead it felfe, ftings more than Nettles;
I have never beene foule mouthd againft thy faw,
Nev'r reveald fecret, for I knew none; would not
Had I kend all that were; I never practifed
Vpon mans wife, nor would the Libells reade
Of liberall wits: I never at great feaftes
Sought to betray a Beautie, but have blufh'd
At fimpring Sirs that did: I have beene harfh
To large Confeffors, and have hotly afh'd them
If they had Mothers, I had one, a woman,
And women t'wer they wrong'd. I knew a man
Of eightie winters, this I told them, who
A Laffe of foureteene brided; twas thy power
To put life into duft, the aged Crampe
Had fcrew'd his fquare foote round,
The Gout had knit his fingers into knots,
Torturing Convulfions from his globie eyes,
Had almoft drawne their fpheeres, that what was life
In him feem'd torture: this Anatomie
Had by his yong faire pheare a Boy, and I
Beleev'd it was his, for fhe fwore it was,
And who would not beleeve her? briefe I am
To thofe that prate and have done; no Companion
To thofe that boaft and have not; a defyer
To thofe that would and cannot; a Rejoycer,
Yea him I doe not love, that tells clofe offices
The fowleft way, nor names concealements in
The boldeft language, fuch a one I am,
And vow that lover never yet made figh
Truer then I. O then moft foft fweet goddeffe

L   Give

Give me the victory of this question, which
Is true loves merit, and blesse me with a signe
Of thy great pleasure.

Here Musicke is heard, Doves are seene to flutter, they
fall againe upon their faces, then on their knees.

Pal. O thou that from eleven, to ninetie raign'st
In mortall bosomes, whose chase is this world
And we in heards thy game; I give thee thankes
For this faire Token, which being layd unto
Mine innocent true heart, armes in assurance   *They bow.*
My body to this businesse: Let us rise
And bow before the goddesse : Time comes on,   *Exeunt.*
                                       Still Musicke of Records.

Enter Emilia *in white, her haire about her shoulders, a whea-*
ten wreath : One in white holding up her traine, her haire
stucke with flowers : One before her carrying a silver
Hynde, in whic his conveyd Incense and sweet odours,
which being set upon the Altar her maides standing a
loofe, she sets fire to it, then they curtsey and kneele.

Emilia. O sacred, shadowie, cold and constant Queene,
Abandoner of Revells, mute contemplative,
Sweet, solitary, white as chaste, and pure
As windefand Snow, who to thy femall knights
Alow'st no more blood than will make a blush,
Which is their orders robe. I heere thy Priest
Am humbled fore thine Altar, O vouchsafe
With that thy rare greene eye, which never yet
Beheld thing maculate, looke on thy virgin,
And sacred silver Mistris, lend thine eare
(Which nev'r heard scurrill terme, into whose port
Ne're entred wanton sound,) to my petition
Seasond with holy feare; This is my last
Of vestall office, I am bride habited,
But mayden harted, a husband I have pointed,
But doe not know him, out of two, I should
Choose one, and pray for his successe, but I
Am guiltlesse of election of mine eyes,
Were I to loose one, they are equall precious,

I could doombe neither, that which perish'd should
too't unfentenc'd: Therefore moft modeft Queene,
He of the two Pretenders, that beft loves me
And has the trueft title in't, Let him
Take off my wheaten Gerland, or elfe grant
The fyle and qualitie I hold, I may
Continue in thy Band.

Here the Hynde vanishes under the Altar: and in the
place afcends a Rofe Tree, having one Rofe upon it.

See what our Generall of Ebbs and Flowes
Out from the bowells of her holy Altar
With facred act advances: But one Rofe,
If well infpir'd, this Battaile fhal confound
Both thefe brave Knights, and I a virgin flowre
Muft grow alone unpluck'd.

Here is heard a fodaine twang of Inftruments, and the
Rofe fals from the Tree.

The flowre is falne, the Tree defcends: O Miftris
Thou here difchargeft me, I fhall be gather'd,
I thinke fo, but I know not thine owne will;
Vnclafpe thy Mifterie: I hope fhe's pleas'd,
Her Signes were gratious.

They curtfey and Exeunt.

Scæna 2. *Enter Doctor, Iaylor and Wooer, in habite of*
Palamon.

Doct. Has this advice I told you, done any good upon her?
Wooer. O very much; The maids that hept her company
Have halfe perfwaded her that I am *Palamon*; within this
Halfe houre fhe came fmiling to me, and asked me what I
Would eate, and when I would kiffe her: I told her
Prefently, and kift her twice.

Doct. Twas well done; twentie times had bin far better,
For there the cure lies mainely.

Wooer. Then fhe told me
She would watch with me to night, for well fhe knew
What houre my fit would take me.

Doct. Let her doe fo,
And when your fit comes, fit her home,

And presently.

Wooer. She would have me sing.

Doctor. You did so?

Wooer. No.

Doct. Twas very ill done then,
You should observe her ev'ry way.

Wooer. Alas
I have no voice Sir, to confirme her that way.

Doctor. That's all one, if yee make a noyse,
If she intreate againe, doe any thing.
Lye with her if she aske you.

Iaylor. Hoa there Doctor.

Doctor. Yes in the waie of cure.

Iaylor But first by your leave
I'th way of honestie.

Doctor. That's but a nicenesse;
Nev'r cast your child away for honestie;
Cure her first this way, then if shee will be honest,
She has the path before her.

Iaylor. Thanke yee Doctor.

Doctor. Pray bring her in
And let's see how shee is.

Iaylor. I will, and tell her.
Her Palamon staies for her : But Doctor,
Me thinkes you are i'th wrong still.   *Exit Iaylor.*

Doct. Goe, goe: you Fathers are fine Fooles: her honesty?
And we should give her physicke till we finde that?

Wooer. Why, doe you thinke she is not honest Sir?

Doctor. How old is she?

Wooer. She's eighteene.

Doctor. She may be,
But that's all one, tis nothing to our purpose,
What ere her Father saies, if you perceave
Her moode inclining that way that I spoke of:
Videlicet, the *way of flesh*, you have me.

Wooer. Yet very well Sir.

Doctor. Please her appetite
And doe it home, it cures her *ipso facto*,

                                        The.

The mellencholly humour that infects her,
  Wooer. I am of your minde *Doctor.*

Enter Iaylor, Daughter, Maide.

  Docter. You'l finde it fo ; fhe comes, pray honour her.
  Iaylor. Come, your Love *Palamon* ftaies for you childe,
And has done this long houre, to vifite you.
  Daughter. I thanke him for his gen'le patience,
He's a kind Gentleman, and I am much bound to him,
Did you nev'r fee the horfe he gave me?
  Iaylor. Yes.
  Daugh. How doe you like him?
  Iaylor. He's a very faire one.
  Daugh. You never faw him dance?
  Iaylor. No.
  Daugh. I have often.
He daunces very finely, very comely,
And for a Iigge, come cut and long taile to him,
He turnes ye like a Top.
  Iaylor. That's fine indeede.
  Daugh. Hee'l dance the Morris twenty mile an houre,
And that will founder the beft hobby-horfe
(If I have any skill) in all the parifh,
And gallops to the turne of *Light a'love,*
What thinke you of this horfe?
  Iaylor. Having thefe vertues
I thinke he might be broght to play at **Tennis.**
  Daugh. Alas that's nothing.
  Iaylor. Can he write and reade too.
  Daugh. A very faire hand, and cafts himfelfe th'accounts
Of all his hay and provender : That Hoftler
Muft rife betime that cozens him ; you know
The Cheftnut Mare the Duke has?
  Iaylor. Very well.
  Daugh. She is horribly in love with him, poore beaft,
But he is like his mafter coy and fcornefull.
  Iaylor. What dowry has fhe?
  Daugh. Some two hundred Bottles,
And twenty ftrike of Oates, but hee'l ne're have her;

He

He lifpes in's neighing able to entice
A Millars Mare,
Hee'l be the death of her.

   Doctor. What ftuffe fhe utters?

   Iaylor. Make curtfie, here your love comes.

   Wooer. Pretty foule
How doe ye? that's a fine maide, ther's a curtfie.

   Daugh. Yours to command ith way of honeftie;
How far is't now to'th end o'th world my Mafters?

   Doctor. Why a daies Iorney wench.

   Daugh. Will you goe with me?

   Wooer. What fhall we doe there wench?

   Daugh. Why play at ftoole ball,
What is there elfe to doe?

   Wooer. I am content
If we fhall keepe our wedding there:

   Daugh. Tis true
For there I will affure you, we fhall finde
Some blind Prieft for the purpofe, that will venture
To marry us, for here they are nice, and foolifh;
Befides my father muft be hang'd to morrow
And that would be a blot i'th bufineffe
Are not you *Palamon*?

   Wooer. Doe not you know me?

   Daugh. Yes, but you care not for me; I have nothing
But this pore petticoate, and too corfe Smockes.

   Wooer. That's all one, I will have you.

   Daugh. Will you furely?

   Wooer. Yes by this faire hand will I.

   Daugh. Wee'l to bed then.

   Wooer. Ev'n when you will.

   Daugh. O Sir, you would faine be nibling.

   Wooer. Why doe you rub my kiffe off?

   Daugh. Tis a fweet one,
And will perfume me finely againft the wedding.
Is not this your Cofen *Arcite*?

   Doctor. Yes fweet heart,
And I am glad my Cofen *Palamon*

Has made so faire a choice.

Daugh. Doe you thinke hee'l have me?

Doctor. Yes without doubt.

Daugh. Doe you thinke so too?

Iaylor. Yes.   (growne,

Daugh. We shall have many children: Lord, how y'ar
My *Palamon* I hope will grow too finely
Now he's at liberty: Alas poore Chicken
He was kept downe with hard meate, and ill lodging
But ile kisse him up againe.

                                        Enter a Messenger.

Mess. What doe you here, you'l loose the noblest sight
That ev'r was seene.

Iaylor. Are they i'th Field?

Mess. They are
You beare a charge there too.

Iaylor. Ile away straight
I must ev'n leave you here.

Doctor. Nay wee'l goe with you,
I will not loose the Fight.

Iaylor. How did you like her?

Doctor. Ile warrant you within these 3. or 4 daies
Ile make her right againe. You must not from her
But still preserve her in this way.

Wooer. I will.

Doc. Lets get her in.

Wooer. Come sweete wee'l goe to dinner
And then weele play at Cardes.

Daugh. And shall we kisse too?

Wooer. A hundred times

Daugh. And twenty.

Wooer. I and twenty.

Daugh. And then wee'l sleepe together.

Doc. Take her offer.

Wooer. Yes marry will we.

Daugh. But you shall not hurt me.

Wooer. I will not sweete.

Daugh. If you doe (Love) ile cry.   *Florish Exeunt.*
                                               Scæna.

Scæna 3. Enter Thesew, Hipolita, Emilia, Perithous : and some Attendants, T. Tucke: Curtis.

Emil. Ile no step further.

Per. Will you loose this sight?

Emil. I had rather see a wren hawke at a fly
Then this decision ev'ry;blow that falls
Threats a brave life, each stroake laments
The place whereon it fals, and sounds more like
A Bell, then blade : I will stay here,
It is enough my hearing shall be punishd,
With what shall happen, gainst the which there is
No deassing, but to heare ; not taint mine eye
With dread sights, it may shun.

Pir. Sir, my good Lord
Your Sister will no further.

Thes. Oh she must.
She shall see deeds of honour in their kinde,
Which sometime show well pencild. Nature now
Shall make, and act the Story, the beleife
Both seald with eye, and eare; you must be present,
You are the victours meede, the price, and garlond
To crowne the Questions title.

Emil. Pardon me,
If I were there, I'ld winke

Thes. You must be there ;
This Tryall is as t'wer i'th night, and you
The onely star to shine.

Emil. I am extinct,
There is but envy in that light, which showes
The one the other: darkenes which ever was
The dam of horrour, who do's stand accurst
Of many mortall Millions, may even now
By casting her blacke mantle over both
That neither could finde other, get her selfe
Some part of a good name, and many a murther
Set off wherto she's guilty.

Hip. You must goe.

Emil. In faith I will not.

                                                          Thes.

Thes. Why the knights must kindle
Their valour at your eye:know of this war
You are the Treasure,and must needes be by
To give the Service pay.

Emil, Sir pardon me,
The tytle of a kingdome may be tride
Out of it selfe.

Thes. Well,well then,at your pleasure,
Those that remaine with you,could wish their office
To any of their Enemies.

Hip. Farewell Sister,
I am like to know your husband fore your selfe
By some small start of time, he whom the gods
Doe of the two know best, I pray them he
Be made your Lot.

　　　　Exeunt Theseus,Hipolita,Perithous,&c.

Emil. *Arcite* is gently visagd; yet his eye
Is like an Engyn bent,or a sharpe weapon
In a soft sheath;mercy,and manly courage
Are bedfellowes in his visage: *Palamon*
Has a most menacing aspect,his brow
Is grav'd,and seemes to bury what it frownes on,
Yet sometime tis not so, but alters to
The quallity of his thoughts; long time his eye
Will dwell upon his object. Mellencholly
Becomes him nobly; So do's *Arcites* mirth,
But *Palamons* sadnes is a kinde of mirth,
So mingled, as if mirth did make him sad,
And sadnes,merry; those darker humours that
Sticke misbecomingly on others,on them
Live in faire dwelling.

　　　　Cornets. Trompets sound as to a charge.
Harke how yon spurs to spirit doe incite
The Princes to their proofe, *Arcite* may win me,
And yet may *Palamon* wound *Arcite* to
The spoyling of his figure. O what pitty
Enough for such a chance; if I were by
I might doe hurt,for they would glance their eies

　　　　M　　　　　　　　　Toward

Toward my Seat, and in that motion might
Omit a ward, or forfeit an offence
Which crav'd that very time : it is much better
(*Cornets. a great cry and noice within crying a Palamon.*)
I am not there, oh better never borne
Then minifter to fuch harme, what is the chance ?

         Enter Servant.

  Ser. The Crie's a *Palamon.*

  Emil. Then he has won: Twas ever likely,
He lookd all grace and fucceffe, and he is
Doubtleffe the prim'ft of men: I pre'thee run
And tell me how it goes.

      Showt, and Cornets: Crying a Palamon.
  Ser. Still *Palamon.*

  Emil. Run and enquire, poore Servant thou haft loft,
Vpon my right fide ftill I wore thy picture,
Palamons on the left, why fo, I know not,
I had no end in't ; elfe chance would have it fo.

    Another cry, and showt within, and Cornets.
On the finifter fide, the heart lyes ; *Palamon*
Had the beft boding chance: This burft of clamour
Is fure th'end o'th Combat.   *Enter Servant.*

  Ser. They faide that *Palamon* had *Arcites* body
Within an inch o'th Pyramid, that the cry
Was generall a *Palamon:* But anon,
Th'Affiftants made a brave redemption, and
The two bold Tytlers, at this inftant are
Hand to hand at it.

  Emil. Were they metamorphifd
Both into one ; oh why ? there were no woman
Worth fo compofd a Man: their fingle fhare,
Their noblenes peculier to them, gives
The prejudice of difparity values fhortnes

      Cornets. Cry within, Arcite, Arcite.
To any Lady breathing———— More exulting ?
Palamon ftill ?

  Ser. Nay, now the found is *Arcite.*

  Emil. I pre'thee lay attention to the Cry.

             Cornets,

Cornets, a great showt and cry, Arcite, victory.
Set both thine eares to'th busines.

Ser. The cry is
Arcite, and victory, harke *Arcite,* victory,
The Combats consummation is proclaim'd
By the wind Instruments.

Emil. Halfe sights saw
That *Arcite* was no babe : god's lyd, his richnes
And costlines of spirit look't through him, it could
No more be hid in him, then fire in flax,
Then humble banckes can goe to law with waters,
That drift windes, force to raging : I did thínke
Good *Palamon* would miscarry, yet I knew not
Why I did thinke so; Our reasons are not prophets
When oft our fancies are: They are comming off :
Alas poore *Palamon.*   *Cornets.*

Enter Theseus, Hipolita, Pirithous, Arcite as victor, and
attendants, &c.

   Thes. Lo, where our Sister is in expectation,
Yet quaking, and unsetled: Fairest *Emily,*
The gods by their divine arbitrament
Have given you this Knight, he is a good one
As ever strooke at head: Give me your hands;
Receive you her, you him, be plighted with
A love that growes, as you decay;

   Arcite. Emily,
To buy you, I have lost what's deerest to me,
Save what is bought, and yet I purchase cheapely,
As I doe rate your value.

   Thes. O loved Sister,
He speakes now of as brave a Knight as ere
Did spur a noble Steed : Surely the gods
Would have him die a Batchelour, least his race
Should shew i'th world too godlike : His behaviour
So charmd me, that me thought *Alcides* was
To him a sow of lead : if I could praise
Each part of him to'th all; I have spoke, your *Arcite*
Did not loose by't ; For he that was, thus good

        M 2   Encountred

Encountred yet his Better, I have heard
Two emulous Philomels, beate the eare o'th night
With their contentious throates, now one the higher,
Anon the other, then againe the first,
And by and by out breasted, that the sence
Could not be judge betweene 'em: So it far'd
Good space betweene these kinesmen; till heavens did
Make hardly one the winner: weare the Girlond
With joy that you have won: For the subdude,
Give them our present Iustice, since I know
Their lives but pinch'em; Let it here be done:
The Sceane's not for our seeing, goe we hence,
Right joyfull, with some sorrow. Arme your prize,
I know you will not loose her: *Hipolita*
I see one eye of yours conceives a teare
The which it will deliver. *Florish.*

   Emil. Is this wynning?
Oh all you heavenly powers where is you mercy?
But that your wils have saide it must be so,
And charge me live to comfort this unfriended,
This miserable Prince, that cuts away
A life more worthy from him, then all women;
I should, and would die too.

   Hip. Infinite pitty
That fowre such eies should be so fixd on one
That two must needes be blinde for't.

   Thes. So it is. *Exeunt.*

Scæna 4. *Enter Palamon and his Knightes pyniond; Iaylor,*
   Executioner &c. Gard.

Ther's many a man alive, that hath out liv'd
The love o'th people, yea i'th selfesame state
Stands many a Father with his childe; some comfort
We have by so considering: we expire
And not without mens pitty. To live still,
Have their good wishes, we prevent
The loathsome misery of age, beguile
The Gowt and Rheume, that in lag howres attend
For grey approachers; we come towards the gods

                             Yong

Yong, and unwapper'd not, halting under Crymes
Many and ftale : that fure fhall pleafe the gods
Sooner than fuch,to give us Nectar with 'em,
For we are more cleare Spirits.   My deare kinfemen.
Whofe lives(for this poore comfort)are laid downe,
You have fould 'em too too cheape.

  1. *K.* What ending could be
Of more content ? ore us the victors have
Fortune,whofe title is as momentary,
As to us death is certaine : A graine of honour
They not ore'-weigh us.

  2. *K.* Let us bid farewell;
And with our patience,anger tottring Fortune,
Who at her certain'ft reeles.

  3. *K.* Come ? who begins ?
  Pal. Ev'n he that led you to this Banket,fhall
Tafte to you all : ah ha my Friend, my Friend,
Your gentle daughter gave me freedome once ;
You'l fee't done now for ever : pray how do'es fhe ?
I heard fhe was not well ; her kind of ill
gave me fome forrow.

  Iaylor. Sir fhe's well reftor'd,
And to be marryed fhortly.

  Pal. By my fhort life
I am moft glad on't ; Tis the lateft thing
I fhall be glad of,pre'thee tell her fo :
Commend me to her,and to peece her portion
Tender her this.

  1. *K.* Nay lets be offerers all.
  2. *K.* Is it a maide ?
  Pal. Verily I thinke fo,
A right good creature,more to me deferving
Then I can quight or fpeake of.

  All K. Commend us to her.   *They give their purfes.*
  Iaylor. The gods requight you all,
And make her thankefull.

  Pal. Adiew; and let my life be now as fhort,
As my leave taking.   *Lies on the Blocke.*

1. *K.* Leade couragiour Cosin.

1.2. *K.* Wee'l follow cheerefully.

A great noise within crying, run, save hold:

Enter in hast a Messenger.

Mess. Hold, hold, O hold, hold, hold.

Enter Pirithous in haste.

Pir. Hold hoa : It is a cursed hast you made

If you have done so quickly : noble *Palamon,*

The gods will shew their glory in a life.

That thou art yet to leade.

Pal. Can that be;

When *Venus* I have said is false ? How doe things fare ?

Pir. Arise great Sir, and give the tydings eare

That are most early sweet, and bitter.

Pal. What

Hath wakt us from our dreame ?

Pir. List then : your Cosen

Mounted upon a Steed that *Emily*

Did first bestow on him, a blacke one, owing

Not a hayre worth of white, which some will say

Weakens his price, and many will not buy

His goodnesse with this note : Which superstition

Heere findes allowance : On this horse is *Arcite*

Trotting the stones of *Athens,* which the *Calkins*

Did rather tell, then trample; for the horse

Would make his length a mile, if't pleas'd his Rider

To put pride in him : as he thus went counting

The flinty pavement, dancing as t'wer to'th Musicke

His owne hoofes made; (for as they say from iron

Came Musickes origen) what envious Flint,

Cold as old *Saturne,* and like him possest

With fire malevolent, darted a Sparke

Or what feirce sulphur else, to this end made,

I comment not; the hot horse, hot as fire

Tooke Toy at this, and fell to what disorder

His power could give his will, bounds, comes on, end,

Forgets schoole doing, being therein traind,

And of kind mannadge, pig-like he whines

At

At the sharpe Rowell, which he freats at rather
Then any jot obaies; seekes all foule meanes
Of boystrous and rough Iadrie, to dif-seate
His Lord, that kept it bravely: when nought serv'd,
When neither Curb would cracke, girth breake nor diffring
Dif-roote his Rider whence he grew, but that   (plunges
He kept him tweene his legges, on his hind hoofes
                                                  on end he stands
That *Arcites* leggs being higher then his head
Seem'd with strange art to hang: His victors wreath
Even then fell off his head: and presently
Backeward the Iade comes ore, and his full poyze
Becomes the Riders loade: yet is he living,
But such a vessell tis, that floates but for
The surge that next approaches: he much desires
To have some speech with you: Loe he appeares.

    Enter Theseus, Hipolita, Emilia, Arcite, in a chaire.

    Pal. O miserable end of our alliance.
The gods are mightie *Arcite*, if thy heart,
Thy worthie, manly heart be yet unbroken:
Give me thy last words, I am *Palamon*,
One that yet loves thee dying.

    Arc. Take *Emilia*
And with her, all the worlds joy: Reach thy hand,
Farewell: I have told my last houre; I was false,
Yet never treacherous: Forgive me Cosen:
One kisse from faire *Emilia*: Tis done:
Take her: I die.

    Pal. Thy brave soule seeke *Elizium.*   (thee,

    Emil. Ile close thine eyes Prince: blessed soules be with
Thou art a right good man, and while I live,
This day I give to teares.

    Pal. And I to honour.

    Thes. In this place first you fought: ev'n very here
I sundred you, acknowledge to the gods
Our thankes that you are living:
His part is play'd, and though it were too short
He did it well: your day is lengthned, and,

                        The

The blissefull dew of heaven do's arowze you.
The powerfull *Venus*, well hath grac'd her Altar,
And given you your love : Our Master *Mars*
Hast vouch'd his Oracle, and to *Arcite* gave
The grace of the Contention : So the Deities
Have shewd due justice : Beare this hence.

Pal. O Cosen,
That we should things desire, which doe cost us
The losse of our desire ; That nought could buy
Deare love, but losse of deare love.

Thes. Never Fortune
Did play a subtler Game : The conquerd triumphes,
The victor has the Losse : yet in the passage,
The gods have beene most equall : *Palamon*,
Your kinseman hath confest the right o'th Lady .
Did lye in you, for you first saw her, and
Even then proclaimd your fancie : He restord her
As your stolne Iewell, and desir'd your spirit
To send him hence forgiven ; The gods my justice
Take from my hand, and they themselves become
The Executioners : Leade your Lady off ;
And call your Lovers from the stage of death,
Whom I adopt my Frinds.   A day or two
Let us looke sadly, and give grace unto
The Funerall of *Arcite*, in whose end
The visages of Bridegroomes weele put on
And smile with *Palamon* ; for whom an houre,
But one houre since, I was as dearely sorry,
As glad of *Arcite* ; and am now as glad,
As for him sorry. O you heavenly Charmers,
What things you make of us ? For what we lacke
We laugh, for what we have, are sorry still,
Are children in some kind.   Let us be thankefull
For that which is, and with you leave dispute
That are above our question : Let's goe off,
And beare us like the time.   *Florish. Exeunt.*

Epilogue.

EPILOGVE.

I Would now aske ye how ye like the Play,
But as it is with Schoole Boyes, cannot say,
I am cruell fearefull : pray yet stay a while,
And let me looke upon ye : No man smile?
Then it goes hard I see; He that has
Lov'd a yong hansome wench then, show his face:
Tis strange if none be heere, and if he will
Against his Conscience let him hisse, and kill
Our Market : Tis in vaine, I see to stay yee,
Have at the worst can come, then; Now what say ye?
And yet mistake me not : I am not bold
We have no such cause. If the tale we have told
(For tis no other) any way content ye)
(For to that honest purpose it was ment ye)
We have our end; and ye shall have ere long
I dare say many a better, to prolong
Your old loves to us : we, and all our might,
Rest at your service, Gentlemen, good night.

Florish.

FINIS.

N